To Dear Jane
With much l[ove]
from Mum.

Women in the Ancient World

Lorna Oakes

Illustrations by Margaret Crutchley.

ISBN: 978-1-907257-45-2

Published by
Quoin Publishing Ltd.,
17 North Street, Middlesbrough,
England TS2 1JP

About the author

After reading for a degree in Ancient History at University College, London, Lorna Oakes taught Egyptology and Near Eastern Studies at Birkbeck College, University of London. As a Special Assistant at the British Museum she has frequently taken part in its programme of public lectures and gallery talks. She has led many successful tours to Egypt, Syria, China and Tibet.

Her publications include *Sacred Sites of Ancient Egypt, The Illustrated Encyclopaedia of Pyramids, Temples and Tombs of Ancient Egypt, Temples and Sacred Sites of Ancient Egypt* and a children's book – *Stories from Herodotus*. She has also produced a children's activity book on the Assyrians for the British Museum as well as several trails and a Teachers' Guide for the use of schools in the Assyrian Galleries.

Dedication

This book is dedicated to my granddaughter Laura Korge.

Acknowledgements

I should like to thank Bob Watson for the interest he showed in this book and for making its publication possible, Margaret Crutchley for her delightful illustrations and also Anna Seager for her map of the Ancient World. My thanks go too to the Images Department of the British Museum for permission to reproduce the Hawara mummy portrait and to Penguin Classics for permission to quote from Euripides, Plutarch and Tacitus.

I am also grateful to my son, Michael, for taking the time to read through the manuscript and for all the support of my friends and family.

Contents

Introduction

Women are very much in the news today with demands for equal pay and almost daily accusations of sexual harassment by former bosses. However, they are also newsworthy because of the great advances that have been made in recent years in the status of women. Although much remains to be done, it is now possible for women to hold senior positions in many aspects of life, in business, politics, medicine and public life. We recently had a woman as Prime Minister and the Commissioner of the Metropolitan Police is a woman. In 2017 the Medical Women's Federation, the largest UK body of women doctors, celebrated one-hundred years of working for the personal and professional development of women in medicine. There are now more women than men entering the medical profession. Women hold some of the top jobs in business and we have women engineers and town planners. Recent research by the BBC has shown, however, that in spite of these improvements, the proportion of women to men in high positions in all these fields is still too low and pressure groups are working hard to try to redress the balance.

This book is mainly about women in the Ancient World who lived at different times and in different places. Some of them were ordinary women whose main job was to look after their families and had little opportunity to work outside the home, although their legal and social status differed from place to place and from time to time. Others became famous for their outstanding qualities of leadership and astute political understanding.

The purpose of this book is to illustrate what life was like for many women in the Ancient World as well as to show what great achievements it was possible for some to accomplish. However, it would be wrong to think that here we have the beginnings of the modern women's movement. What we do have is only a number of isolated examples. Even today in some areas women have only recently got the vote, while even the remarkable women of the past made little impact on history beyond their own lifetime, but they do show what women can do if they set their mind to it. At the United Nations women's conference in 2015 Meghan Markle spoke about women's role in the world. She said that girls with dreams become women of vision and urged women to empower each other to bring about change. As she says, if we empower women we empower the next generation too. So let's get to work!

THE MIDDLE EAST

Statuette of a Sumerian woman.

She is shown praying and the figure comes from a temple in Mesopotamia (c.2400 BC).

Chapter 1

Women of Mesopotamia

Mesopotamia is Ancient Iraq. The name means 'Between the Rivers', the rivers being the Tigris and Euphrates. It includes all the land between them from Turkey and Syria in the north to the Gulf in the south. Throughout the long history of the area it is difficult to find out what it was like to be a woman living in the various societies which developed at different periods in different places. The evidence which is available is patchy and applies only to particular times and places. It is impossible to describe a woman's life all over Mesopotamia all of the time.

From around 3000 – 2000 BC the south of the area was called Sumer. Sumer was not a country but a collection of independent city-states each with its own king and own protective god. It is hard to find out very much about women at this time as they are not often mentioned in texts or depicted in works of art, apart from temple figurines where they are shown as worshippers, as are contemporary men. Uruinimgina, the king of the city-state of Lagash, mentioned them in his so-called Reforms which he issued when he came to the throne. He says he solemnly promised his god, Ningirsu, he would never subject the widow or the orphan to the powerful, so some women at least had some protection in society. Nonetheless it seems to have been a man's world as another of his 'reforms' says that a woman found guilty of speaking disrespectfully to a man shall have her mouth crushed with a baked brick! And the brick should be displayed at the city gate (as a clear warning to any other woman thinking of speaking her mind!).

A better impression is given in the cuneiform texts found at Kanesh in modern Turkey. These are letters written about 1900 BC during the Old Assyrian period between family members engaged in business in Anatolia (modern Turkey). They describe a thriving trade in textiles and tin organized by the influential merchant banking families based in Ashur, an important city in Northern Iraq on the River Tigris. Women were often left in charge of the family business while the men were away. Others produced the textiles to be sold and received payment for their work.

Donkey loads of these commodities went up through the mountain passes to Kanesh (near modern Kaiseri) where they were exchanged for silver. The journey took five to six weeks in each direction so husbands were away for long periods of time, especially if they went on from Kanesh to other towns and trading posts to sell their goods. Sometimes women went along as well but had to have a male relative as chaperone. At least one woman went to Kanesh and further afield, the idea being that she accompanied her husband on his business trips. However, she seems to have had difficulty in catching up with him. Every time she arrived at the place he told her to meet him she found he'd gone off somewhere else. She complained bitterly about this:

> *You left me in Purushhaddum and I really felt it was a case of out of sight out of mind! Even now when I have come all the way here to Hahhum you are not looking after me. In Kanesh you insulted me and for a whole year would not let me come to your bed. From Timilkiya you wrote to me, 'If you don't come here you are no longer my wife! I will make things worse than in Purushhaddum.' Then you went from Timilkiya to Kanesh saying, 'I will leave again from Kanesh within 15 days,' but instead of 15 days you stayed one year. You wrote to me from Kanesh, 'Come up to Hahhum.' So now I have been living in Hahhum for a year and you do not even mention my name in your business letters.*

However, other letters make it clear that women were very important to the trade. Textiles were the most valuable commodity to be sold in Anatolia and they were produced by the women of Ashur. The men kept an eye out for what was in fashion at any one moment and so in what direction their profit lay. Puzur-Ashur wrote to his wife, Waqqurtum:

Concerning that fine cloth you sent me you must make me some more like that and send it to me with Ashur-idi and then I will send you half a pound of silver per piece as payment. Have one side of the cloth combed, but not shaved smooth. It should be close textured. Compared to the textiles you sent me earlier, you must work in one pound of wool more per piece of cloth, but it must still be fine. The other side of the cloth must be just lightly combed. If it still looks hairy it will have to be close shaved. Don't send me any more of that Abarne cloth. If you don't want to make any fine cloth, buy some! I hear there is plenty to be had in Ashur. A finished piece of cloth should be 9 ells long and 8 ells wide (4.5 x 4 m).

Some wives put pressure on their husbands to come back to Ashur and pay up. One wife, and possibly her sister, complained about the length of time the merchant had been away. They had seen neither hide nor hair of him for months. They said he ought to come back and pay his respects to the gods. However, their real reason for wanting him to return is revealed in the last sentence of their letter to him: '*And what about the money for our textiles?*'

Another woman wrote to her son asking him to come back to Ashur quickly so she could return to Kanesh with him and rescue the family business. She must have been quite a formidable woman and forcefully reminded him of his obligations to the family firm now that his father was too frail to control affairs.

Several of the letters found at Kanesh were written by or to women. One wife complained bitterly that her husband had gone away on business and left her without the means of supporting herself. She writes:

You told me to keep the bracelets and rings that I already have as I will need them to buy food. It is true that you sent me half a pound of gold through Ili-bani (one of the businessmen) but where are these bracelets and rings (you are on about)? When you left you didn't leave me anything. You cleaned the house out completely and took everything with you.

Since you left a terrible famine has broken out in Ashur ...and I need to buy barley for food...what is this extravagance you mention? We have absolutely nothing to eat!…Make sure you send me the value of my textiles in silver so I can at least buy ten measures of barley.

Another was written by a prospective bridegroom and shows that marriages were arranged rather like a business transaction and that the girl's father had to agree before she could marry. The letter doesn't mention the girl's views on the subject although it does say what her duties will be!

Puzur-Ashur says; tell Nuhshatum:
Your father has written to me about you suggesting that I should marry you. I have sent my servants and a letter regarding you so that he will let you come. I am asking you, the moment you read my letter, ask your father (for permission) and come here with my servants. I am alone, I have no one to get my dinner ready for me or set my table. If you don't come with my servants I will marry a young girl from Wahshushana. Take notice! Get a move on and come at once!

Some of the merchants who lived for considerable periods in Kanesh did marry local girls and started a family even though they already had a wife and children back in Ashur. There were no legal or moral taboos on this practice provided the two women did not live in the same city. Usually only the one who lived in Ashur was considered to be the 'wife' while the local girl was described as 'consort'. Otherwise neither the Assyrians nor the local people practised bigamy. Apparently it was only the prospect of a wealthy businessman as a 'good catch' that allowed them to stretch a point.

In the south of Ancient Iraq lay the city of Babylon. One of the most famous kings of Babylon was Hammurabi who also controlled some of the surrounding cities in the eighteenth century BC. He is also famous for his so-called Law Code. The laws are written on a large piece of black stone now in the Louvre Museum in Paris. Some of them discuss marriage. It seems that weddings were long-drawn-out affairs. In the first place gifts of garments, silver and a ring were sent by the girl's father to the bridegroom. Then offerings had to be made in the temples of the couple's home towns. The families of the couple exchanged gifts of food. Then the groom's family visited the bride's family and his mother performed some ceremony in the temple and took part in the ritual bathing of the bride and the anointing with oil of her head. After she and other family members went home the groom finally went into the bride's house and stayed there for four months with four of his friends. After this the bride was taken to her new home to live with her husband and his family.

The code also reveals quite a lot about women who played a part in the temple ritual. Some of them could get married, but were not allowed to have children. These women were allowed to give their husband a slave girl to have a baby on her behalf. Another group of texts, from Sippar, mentions women called *naditu*. They lived in a sort of nunnery in Sippar and never got married. The girls came from high-class families; some were priestesses from other states nearby. They were dedicated to the sun-god, Shamash, and 'betrothed' to him and brought 'dowries' with them when they came to the cloister. Possibly they also changed their name when they became part of this religious community. Then they lived with their servants in a house inside the 'nunnery' walls. Their main duty was to pray for their families but they also engaged in business and the profits were added to their dowries. When the *naditu* died these were returned to their respective families, although a *naditu* could and did leave property to anyone she wished. Although she was not allowed to marry she could adopt a daughter and often left property to her in her will. She remained on close terms with her family and was dependent on them for support.

Strangely enough, although the Assyrian palaces of the great kings of the first millennium BC were lavishly decorated with painted carved reliefs very few depict women. Apart from Ashurbanipal's wife, Queen Labbali-sharrat, the only women shown in the reliefs are refugees and prisoners. A typical scene includes a mother giving her child a drink in a long line of captives being presented to the king. Others show mothers, their children and as many household goods as they can take with them piled onto the family camel or oxcart, led by the father, and being taken away into captivity, often hundreds of miles from home.

Sometimes women prisoners would be sold as slaves. There was a great demand for slaves from the heads of wealthy families who saw them as status symbols. They would be employed as domestic workers in their owner's house.

Sometimes the owner would have a child with a slave, usually if he and his wife had not been able to have a son, but the husband had to have his wife's consent.

Between 664 and 648 BC the Assyrian kings often made war on Elam (in S.W. Iran). The wars are recorded in the king's annals (his year-by-year account of the campaigns he had fought) and in the decoration on his palace walls. Some documents regarding private people also often provide information about the wars and their outcome. One such text talks about the fate of one female captive and her daughter. They were regarded as part of the booty seized in Elam and sold as slaves when they reached Ashur. They were originally given to ten men who owned them jointly and who shared the sale price between them after the two were sold. The relevant text is a legal document and reveals that the mother's name was Nanaya-ila'i, but her daughter's is not known, which probably means she was very young and dependent on her mother. They were bought by Mannu-ki-Ashur and worked as domestic servants in his house. They would have had to grind grain to make flour, to do the baking and cooking, as well as the cleaning and may even have had to do some spinning and weaving as part of the household economy. At least they were able to stay together and were not bought by different owners and taken to separate households.

Some of the greatest Assyrian kings lived in the Assyrian Empire period (roughly about 900 – 600 BC). At this time Assyria grew from what had begun as the small city-state of Ashur on the River Tigris to a vast empire which stretched from modern Turkey and Syria in the north to the Gulf in the south and from the Zagros Mountains in the east to the Mediterranean in the west. The kings lived in huge palaces in the capital cities of Nimrud and Nineveh and their exploits are known through the painted carved reliefs which decorated their palace walls and from their written accounts of the battles they fought. Strangely enough very little is known about queens. Only the wife of Ashurbanipal is depicted in reliefs from his palace at Nineveh where she is seen joining in the celebration of his victory over Elam (S.W. Iran). Not even the names of some of them are known, although more have come to light with the discovery in 1988 of the treasures in the tomb of one of Esarhaddon's queens below the palace of Nimrud.

What is known is that the kings had several wives but it is far from clear whether they were all married to the king at the same time. Sennacherib had three wives. Did the king only take another wife when one died? Or if one fell out of favour? If they were all queen at more or less the same time what was their relative status? Was one a principal wife? Were they ranked in order of age? Was it possible for an older queen to 'retire'?

Queens certainly seem to have become more important after they had produced a son. In Assyria the reigning king's eldest son did not necessarily become the next king. Sennacherib's youngest son was proclaimed heir. So why was he chosen? Was he the son of his favourite wife? Whatever the reason, and even though the heir was supposed to have been chosen by the gods, this practice could cause a lot of trouble. Sennacherib was murdered by his jealous older sons and it took Esarhaddon two years of fighting before he was able to take the throne.

Nonetheless, some queens had a great deal of influence. Esarhaddon chose his son, Ashurbanipal, to be his heir to the throne of Assyria, and his brother (maybe his twin) to take the throne of the neighbouring state of Babylon when Esarhaddon himself died. Determined to avoid the civil strife surrounding his own succession he wanted to make sure things went smoothly when the time came, so he drew up treaties to ensure his wishes were carried out.

On the day Esarhaddon, king of Assyria, your lord passes away, (on that day) Ashurbanipal, the great crown prince designate, son of Esarhaddon, your lord, shall be your king and your lord...You shall listen to whatever he says and do whatever he commands, and you shall not seek any other king.

Courtiers and representatives from all over the empire had to swear to keep the terms of the treaties. When Esarhaddon died suddenly on his way to deal with the rebellious Egyptians, Naqi'a-Zakutu, his mother, and grandmother of the two crown princes, made the courtiers and other officials swear again to be loyal to Ashurbanipal and his brother, Shamash-sum-ukin.

It is not known where the queens came from. That they were very wealthy women is obvious from the beautiful jewellery found in the Nimrud tombs in 1988 and a text found with them shows that they came from noble families in Assyria, at least in the ninth century BC. Such information is not available later on but is likely to apply then also. The queens had their own households within the main royal palace and also owned large estates. Their households were run by a *shakintu*, a wealthy woman of high status, and included a deputy *shakintu*, a female scribe, a cook and confectioners.

If the queen outlived her husband she became Queen Mother to the reigning king. This gave her enormous status and influence although no actual power.

Very unusually, one queen mother, Shamu-rammat, went on campaign with the king. This was quite unheard of in Assyrian history. She also had her own stela (commemorative stone) with her name and titles on it in the famous row of other powerful officials' stelae at Ashur. She was such an outstanding woman that many legends grew up around her name where she is called Semiramis.

Chapter 2

Women of the Palace of Mari

Mari was a large city in ancient times. It lay on the great river Euphrates in modern Syria. There was a flourishing palace there in the nineteenth century BC. Almost the whole of it has been excavated. It was a huge building covering over 2.5 hectares. It was mostly built of mud brick as were the walls which entirely surrounded it. There was an impressive entrance which was paved with baked brick and had an imposing tower on either side. Inside the palace the rooms were grouped around large courtyards which seem to have contained gardens. At least one was planted with palm trees. There was a throne room and audience hall where foreign dignitaries would have been received by the king, Zimri-Lim. The internal walls were plastered and painted, sometimes with plain red dadoes with black skirting areas and white for the upper parts, but with beautiful frescoes for the ceremonial areas.

First and foremost the palace was where the royal family lived so it contained their private apartments as well as public areas. It was also a centre of government to which the reports of officials who lived in other towns or other parts of the city of Mari were brought. Some of the courtyards were used for trade. They were big enough to accommodate large numbers of men and the animals needed to transport their goods. The palace was locked at night and provided security for the luxury goods the merchants had for sale. One of the courtyards was used as a bazaar. Because security was tight tax was collected there – one text says in the king's bedroom! Elsewhere wine and dried vegetables were stored in sealed rooms.

The palace was also an industrial centre. Textiles were produced there at least as far as spinning, weaving and sewing were concerned, although dyeing and fulling which are very smelly processes were probably done outside the palace walls. Metalwork was brought into the palace from outside, apparently, as no furnaces have been found inside the palace area. The smelting of bronze would probably also have offended the sensitive noses of the occupants.

A great deal is known about life in the palace from the enormous archives which have been found on the site. The documents were not written on paper or papyrus as you might think, but on clay tablets. These were small cushion-shaped pieces of clay and the writing was done with a stylus pressed into the clay while it was still damp. The script was done in a series of wedges, arranged in different ways and is called cuneiform. The word comes from the Latin word 'cuneus' which means 'wedge'. Generally speaking each group of wedges represented a syllable and you built up words like you do when playing charades. Sometimes whole words could be written with just one group of wedges without any building up. The language used was Akkadian. No one speaks this now but it is a sort of ancestor of modern Hebrew and Arabic.

The archaeologists found thousands of these clay tablets when the palace was excavated last century. The letters concerned every area of palace life and were stored in boxes and baskets in sealed rooms. Strict records were kept of goods coming into the palace and the people who brought them. There were lists of palace staff, reports from elsewhere concerning the movement of foreign troops, records of disputes between members of staff and letters from the king keeping his wife informed of his doings when he was away and many more. Most of these concern men but the letters also reveal a huge amount of information about the women of Mari too.

The letters which passed between King Zimri-Lim and his wife, Queen Shiatsu, are particularly well preserved. Shiatsu was the daughter of the king and queen of Aleppo. She and Zimri-Lim had at least eleven daughters who were married off to other local kings and princes to ensure the loyalty of other states or to put the seal on alliances. In other words they were used as pawns in international politics, a common practice in the ancient world. Strangely there is not much information about sons although one letter Shiatsu wrote to Zimri-Lim says,

'I have given birth to twins, a boy and a girl; may my lord rejoice!'

It may seem rather odd to us today that she wrote a letter to her husband to tell him the news when he lived in the same palace, but it shows the importance of letters and how they were passed continually from one wing of the palace to another and concerned a wide variety of subjects.

It is not known whether the twins survived or not. One letter records the death of a daughter, but which one is not known. One official writes to another saying,

'Before the king reaches Mari, tell him that that daughter is dead, and may he understand; perhaps if the king were not to hear about the death of that daughter until he reaches Mari he might be too distressed.'

Zimri-Lim had a son called Yahdun-Lim but he died. One of the texts records gifts of a silver head-band weighing about four grams and a silver ring weighing about eight grams *for the grave of Yahdun-Lim, the king's son'*.

The tablets show Shibtu as a model wife, always concerned for his well-being. In one letter she writes,

'May my lord conquer his enemies and enter Mari in peace and joy of heart! Now may my lord put on the tunic and coat that I have made.'

She wrote to him all the time, sometimes just to say, *'Mari, the temples and the palace are well'*, but at others she wrote in detail about prophecies or omens that might affect his welfare, or about provisions for the palace kitchens and storerooms, or how prisoners of war were to be employed in the palace workshops. Queen she might be but she didn't just sit around all day enjoying a life of ease and privilege. She had to work hard overseeing all the departments of the palace and often having to settle disputes between the various officials.

One such dispute was about the provision of garments for the palace workers.

Bahdi-Lim, an official in charge of one of the workshops writes,

I have been looking into the matter of the palace workers. Of the 400 palace workers 100 have been given clothes. 'Now what about the other 300?' I asked Mukannishtum. He replied saying, 'This is not my department. Ask Bali-Elah to supply them'. And Bali-Elah replied saying, 'I have given clothes to 100 of the workers. 100 is all I'm supposed to supply and Mukannishtum should supply the rest'. Tricky!

On the other hand Zimri-Lim obviously regarded her highly and always kept her informed about his movements when he was away from Mari.

'As I send this letter to you, I have received the people of the town of Shenah and have made them swear allegiance to me. I have installed a governor in the citadel. After I finish this letter I will depart for Urkish and promote goodwill. Then straight away I will proceed from Urkish to Shuna and promote goodwill there. I am well and my troops are well. May news of the palace reach me regularly.'

Shibtu was not shut away in the palace all the time. In one letter Zimri-Lim asks her to come to meet him as he comes back to Mari after a long absence.

When Shibtu wrote to her husband she usually addressed him as 'My Lord' and called herself 'Shibtu, your servant', although occasionally she calls herself 'Lady of the Land', which definitely means 'Queen'. The letters from his daughters show real affection, however. They call him, 'My father, my star' and sign themselves 'your daughter'.

The queen had help with her large family. The babies would have a wet-nurse and the older children a nanny or governess. Other women had to take their children to work with them and the lists of food rations given as payment show that the mothers got a little extra for their children. These women were employed as spinners and weavers in the palace textile industry.

Women worked in the kitchens at Mari preparing food. A somewhat fierce lady called Ama-dugga was in charge and a kitchen maid, Eliza, was responsible for a drink called *himrum* and the jars in which it was stored. She was also good at making *pappasum* pudding and got an extra allowance of barley for making it.

One letter from Zimri-Lim to Shibtu asked her to select some beautiful young girls from a batch of new prisoners to train as singers, probably to take part in temple ceremonies. It is likely they also played musical instruments. They were paid in amounts of grain and wine along with the king's other serving girls. One ration list says there were thirty-five senior lady musicians, fourteen junior and seven very junior female musicians. The seniors and juniors got the same amounts of food and drink but the very junior ones got less.

Some women acted as midwife for others just as they did in our grandmothers' and great-grandmothers' time in Britain, but one woman, surprisingly, was a doctor. She was definitely a doctor and not a midwife because the words for the two professions are quite different. Medicine was often connected with magic in the ancient world, but at Mari quite a bit was known about purely medical matters. One letter from Zimri-Lim to his wife tells her how a woman with an infectious disease was to be treated:

'I have heard Nanna has an infection, and since she is often at the palace it might infect the many women who are with her. Now give strict orders: no one is to drink from the cup she drank from; no one is to sit on the chair she sat on; and no one is to lie on the bed she lay on, lest it infect the other women who are with her. This is a very contagious disease.'

Another surprise regarding women was to find that at Mari some of the secretaries were women. No details are known about them or the type of work they were given to do or their place in society. They are just names on ration lists, but they are certainly female names and there were nine of them, enough to show that literacy was not the monopoly of men in the palace of Zimri-Lim at Mari.

Chapter 3

Shammu-rammat/Semiramis – Queen of Assyria

Shammu-ramat was a real person. She was an important Assyrian queen, the daughter-in-law of Shalmaneser III, the wife of Shamshi-Adad V and mother of Adad-nirari III. She was so famous, many legends grew up about her and the historians of Ancient Greece wrote accounts of her miraculous birth and her many exploits. In these stories she is called Semiramis.

It used to be thought that Shammu-rammat's son was still a child when he came to the throne and that Shammu-rammat ruled as regent on his behalf rather like Hatshepsut and Thutmose III, her stepson. However, there is no contemporary evidence that she did this, nor that Adad-nirari was so young. Modern historians no longer think this is true although this view is still repeated by some. The real reason for her fame is not known, but it may be connected with the fact she was able to calm civil unrest when her husband died and thus enabled her son to take up his position as king, much as Naqi'a Zakutu's influence secured the situation for Ashurbanipal. However this may be, she was certainly a formidable woman. The Greek historian, Herodotus, who calls her Semiramis, says she was a queen of Babylon and constructed 'some remarkable embankments in the plain outside the city to control the river which until then used to flood the entire countryside'.

The main source of information about her is another Greek historian, Diodorus Siculus, who wrote in the first century BC. He says that Semiramis was semi-divine because her mother was the Syrian fish goddess, Derceto, who fell in love with a mortal, a very handsome young man, and had a daughter by him. When the child was born Derceto killed the young man and left the baby to die in the desert. Then filled with grief and shame at what she had done she threw herself into a nearby lake where her body was changed into a fish although she kept a human face. Fortunately for the baby there were a great many doves nesting nearby and they nurtured her 'in an astounding and miraculous manner'. Some of the doves kept her warm by covering her with their wings and others brought milk in their beaks and kept her alive by dripping it into her mouth drop by drop. They got the milk from a dairy close by when the workers were not looking. When the baby was about a year old the doves decided she needed more substantial food so they went back to the dairy and stole some cheese. The workers realised something strange was going on when they saw the cheeses had been nibbled round the edges so they decided to investigate and found out about the child who was outstandingly beautiful. They took her to the royal herdsman whose name was Simmas. He adopted her as he had no children of his own and called her Semiramis – a name which is very like the Syrian word for 'doves'.

When she had grown up and become a very beautiful young woman an officer came from the court of King Ninus of Assyria to inspect the royal herds. He was called Onnes and when he saw how beautiful Semiramis was he begged Simmas to allow him to marry her. He took her off to his home and had two sons with her. Apparently she was as clever as she was beautiful and her husband was so enslaved by her he never did anything without taking her advice.

King Ninus had by now finished building the city he named after himself (which we call Nineveh) and decided he would go to war against Bactria with an enormous army. Diodorus sometimes consulted the work of yet another Greek historian, Ctesias, to get his information and here it seems that Ctesias had confused the war of King Ninus with that of the Persian king, Xerxes.

Xerxes also assembled a huge army, in this case, to invade Greece. Diodorus' description of Ninus' army sounds much like Herodotus' description of Xerxes' army in *The Histories*. Both kings called up a huge army of thousands if not millions of troops from all parts of their empires.

Ninus had a great struggle to conquer Bactria. At first he was unable to make any headway. His strategy was to send his army contingent by contingent into battle and the Bactrians easily defeated them. Later Ninus changed his tactics and allowed the whole army to swarm into the country. Then it was the turn of the Bactrians to flee. However, although Ninus had taken the country of Bactria he could not capture the main city. Onnes, now on campaign with Ninus, decided the only thing to do was to send for Semiramis. She disguised herself in a garment that made it impossible to tell whether she was a woman or a man and set off on an incredibly long journey. When she arrived she could see at once that Ninus was tackling the problem in entirely the wrong way. He was fighting on the plains where it was easy for the Bactrians to defeat him. She told him to attack the rocky acropolis as it had been left unattended by the guards who had gone down to help their soldiers on the plain. The plan worked and Ninus was so taken with Semiramis that he asked Onnes to release her from his marriage to him and give her to Ninus instead. The king offered his own daughter in exchange. Onnes accepted with such ill grace that Ninus threatened to put his eyes out if he didn't agree. At this Onnes was beside himself, went mad, put a rope round his neck and hanged himself. Ninus now married Semiramis and so she became a queen.

After the capture of the city Ninus took away huge amounts of treasure and disbanded his army. Then he and Semiramis had a son called Ninyas after which he died and his wife became Queen of Assyria and ruled all the lands which he had conquered. This was most unusual as it never before had been heard of that a woman could hold such a position.

Semiramis buried Ninus in the palace precinct and erected over the grave a huge mound that could be seen for miles around. According to Diodorus it could still be seen in his day even though Nineveh had been burned to the ground when the Medes (and Babylonians) had destroyed the Assyrian empire centuries before.

The new queen was a very ambitious woman and keen to become famous for her great exploits so she decided to build a new city in Babylonia (in the south of modern Iraq). This city was called Babylon. After arranging for all the best architects and craftsmen in the world to work on the project, she summoned two-million men from all over her empire to complete the project. She diverted the River Euphrates so that it now flowed through the city, dividing it in half, and built a massive wall with towers at regular intervals to protect it. The walls were said to be so wide two chariots could pass each other along the road on top. She is also credited with having constructed a cleverly engineered bridge across the narrowest part of the river. On each side of the river she also built an expensive quay. Within the city itself she built two lavishly decorated palaces and a temple to Bel, the Babylonian Zeus. Although it was a ruin by Diodorus' time he says all historians agree that it had once been a very tall building, so tall in fact that the Babylonians could study the stars from the top. As if this wasn't enough she also had a reservoir made at the lowest point in Babylonia. She diverted the Euphrates into it and thus made it possible to build an underground passage which connected one palace with the other, so even when she let the river back into its bed she could cross without having to be ferried over.

Full of admiration for her as Diodorus was, he concedes she was not responsible for the famous Hanging Gardens of Babylon. According to him they were constructed to please one of the concubines of a later Syrian king. She was a Persian lady who missed the mountains of her homeland and had asked the king to make her an artificial one. However, Semiramis did build several other towns along the Tigris and Euphrates to encourage trade.

After completing her building operations she decided to visit the other parts of her empire. She set off with an impressive army in the direction of Media.

Diodorus writes that when she reached a mountain called Bagistanus, she encamped near it and laid out a great park which was watered by a nearby spring. The mountain is very high with steep cliffs overlooking the park. The lowest part she smoothed off and had carved on it a figure of herself with a hundred spearmen by her side. She also put an inscription on the cliff in Syrian letters which said:

Semiramis, with the pack-saddles of the beasts of burden in her army, built up a mound from the plain and thereby climbed this precipice even to the very ridge.

The classical writers seem to have confused her exploits with those of other famous leaders. The mountain she calls Bagistanus is actually called Behistun and the inscription is nothing to do with Semiramis. The Behistun Inscription was put there by the Persian king, Darius the Great, and records his defeat of his enemies who tried to prevent him coming to the throne.

After that she went on to Persia and every other country she ruled throughout Asia building fine roads and founding cities wherever she went. Again, the Greek historians are probably confusing her achievements with those of the Persian kings. The cities are likely to refer to Parsagadae, Persepolis and Susa where the palaces of the Persian kings were. Diodorus says many of the works she built throughout Asia are called Works of Semiramis to this day. Even if she is being given credit where none is due these statements reveal the esteem in which she was held in Classical times.

After this she visited Egypt and went to consult the oracle of Ammon at Siwa. Maybe this is also a dim recollection of the fact that Alexander went to the same oracle where he claims he was recognised as the son of Zeus. However this may be, Semiramis is said to have been told by the oracle *that she would disappear from among men and receive undying honour among some of the people of Asia. This would happen when her son, Ninyas, should conspire against her*. Nothing daunted and anxious to achieve military fame she then made plans to invade India, the largest country in the world at that time.

When her spies told her that the Indian king had a far larger army than she had and that he used elephants in warfare she sent urgent messages to all the governors of the places under her control telling them to send troops with new suits of armour. She also sent to Phoenicia, Syria and Cyprus asking for timber to build boats that could be used on the River Indus. And having no real elephants she set about ordering her men to make models, thinking these would scare the Indians because they thought no elephants existed anywhere in the world but India! So she set about her task. She chose 300,000 black oxen, killed them and gave the meat to the craftsmen, but the hides she had sewn together and stuffed with straw, making exact copies of real elephants. Each of the dummies had a man and a camel inside it. When the camel moved it would look from a distance as if an elephant was approaching.

When the Indian king heard about these doings he made strenuous efforts to build an even larger army and navy. He also sent her a letter accusing her of being an aggressor as he had never done her any harm and threatening to crucify her after he had won. Semiramis scornfully replied that *it will be in deeds that the Indian will make trial of my valour.* At first Semiramis gained the upper hand but then the Indian king played a trick on her. He pretended to retreat so as to lure Semiramis and her army across the Indus. Semiramis then spanned the river with a pontoon bridge and leaving 60,000 men to guard it she led the main part of her army in pursuit of the Indians. In the forefront were the dummy elephants who at first did scare the enemy, but then some of the troops left behind gave the game away and told the Indians that they were only dummies. A fierce battle ensued but at last Semiramis was defeated. The remnants of her army fled and the Indian king attacked her personally. He fired an arrow but only scratched her arm; then he attacked her with a javelin but again not much harm was done so she managed to escape to the bridge. Unfortunately, there was such a stampede of soldiers trying to cross many were trampled underfoot. When at last as many as possible had crossed, Semiramis cut the bridge adrift so none of the Indians could get over. The Indian king did not try to cross because he had been advised not to in a dream. So, after exchanging prisoners, Semiramis made her way back to Bactria with the loss of two-thirds of her army.

Some time later her son, Ninyas, conspired against her, but instead of punishing him she turned the kingdom over to him, remembering the prophecy of the oracle of Ammon. She then disappeared as if she were going to join the gods as the oracle had foretold. Some say she turned into a dove and flew off with a great flock of birds which alighted on her house. This, they say, is why the Assyrians worship the dove as a god, thus deifying Semiramis. Diodorus concludes by saying, *'Be that as it may, this woman after having been queen over all Asia, with the exception of India, passed away in the manner described above, having lived sixty-two years and having reigned for forty-two years.'*

In spite of all these stories about her achievements Semiramis had a very bad reputation in later times. It was probably very difficult for men to accept that a woman could do such things and instead she was presented as a 'typical' woman. She was accused of being a scheming, ruthless person, her husband's murderer and having an unseemly sexual appetite. This view of her probably was inspired by Diodorus' story of how she managed to hang on to her power. After her husband's death she had no wish to marry again as she was afraid her new consort might try to take over and deprive her of her power, but she pretended she was wanting to find a new husband. She would choose the most handsome of her soldiers and would spend the night with him but in the morning would have him put to death. Apparently she made a habit of this and thus gained her reputation as an immoral woman.

Over time the story of Semiramis was elaborated and embellished. The Roman writer, Valerius Maximus, mentions the legend that Semiramis was brushing her hair when she was interrupted by a messenger bringing her news of a revolt in Babylon. She rushed out of the palace to deal with it personally, killed the leaders and then went back to the palace to finish her hair-do!

From the Mediaeval period onwards she is presented as a wicked woman, by Chaucer in the *Canterbury Tales (The Monk's Tale)* and Dante in *The Inferno* where she burns in the Hell of the Sins of Lust, although to be fair, Boccaccio admires her achievements as well as condemning her sexual appetite.

In the Renaissance she was sometimes depicted as a Venus figure, associated, with her, for example, in Botticelli's painting of Spring, although the other side of her personality is referred to in Guercino's picture of her receiving news of the revolt of Babylon. Later still she continued to fascinate and Degas painted her looking over her newly built city of Babylon.

Operas have also been composed about her. Verdi's *Semiramide* was first performed in Venice in 1823 and was itself based on Voltaire's play, *Semiramis*. And so on into modern times when interest in her was rekindled by the archaeological discoveries in Assyria (mid-19th century) and at Babylon in the early twentieth. It was during this period that the connection between the legendary Semiramis and the historical Shammu-rammat was made. Unfortunately, there is little about Shammu-ramat in Assyrian sources, so it is difficult to say exactly why she was so important and what there is, is rather boring compared to the exotic tales surrounding the name of Semiramis, so it is not surprising that the traditions about her are the ones which still continue to survive.

EGYPT

Sketch of an Egyptian woman feeding her baby.
From the craftsmen's village at Deir el-Medina (probably Dynasty XIX).

Chapter 4

The Women of Deir el-Medina

It is quite difficult to find information about women in Ancient Egypt. They are mainly known as some man's mother, wife or daughter. On the other hand it is fairly easy to find out about the lives of men because they often wrote their life stories on the walls of their tombs. Women do not seem to have done this, probably because they usually shared the tomb with their husband.

However, one exception to this rule is the village of Deir el-Medina on the West Bank of the River Nile not far from the Valley of the Kings. This was in existence from about 1500-1100BC and was where the craftsmen lived who created the royal tombs of the New Kingdom period. They were highly skilled, the best craftsmen in the land in fact, and they lived here with their wives and children in houses which the government provided for them. They were also paid by the state. Their wages came in the form of food as there was no money at that time.

Their big problem was water. The village was situated in the desert beyond the fertile strip of agricultural land down by the Nile which was about two miles away. All the water had to be brought up from the river in pottery jars or bags made from animal skins on the backs of donkeys. The villagers had several attempts to dig a well at the far end of the village but never managed to succeed. They dug an enormous hole about 25 metres wide and over 50 metres deep, down to well below the water table but it never filled up with water. After giving up on this project they used the hole as the village rubbish dump.

This was very fortunate for the archaeologists who excavated the village in the early twentieth century because the Great Pit, as it came to be known, was full of limestone chippings and bits of broken pottery which the villagers had used as scrap-paper for writing notes to each other, sending bills for work done on houses or tombs belonging to the inhabitants, for registers of people who hadn't turned up for work and the reasons why not, lists of rations for the workers (like modern payslips), accounts of court cases and even wills. These showed that women had equal rights with men. They could own property and had the same legal rights even though they were usually financially dependent on their husbands as they had little opportunity to earn much of an income.

The houses of the village went with the job, so as long as their husbands were employed on the royal tombs the women had a roof over their heads, but if a man was no longer able to work or if the couple divorced, the wife would then be in a precarious position. Sometimes she would be lucky enough to be able to go back to her family and her father would look after her.

One text said that one of the workmen assured his daughter that if her husband threw her out she could come home and live in the portico of his storehouse because it belonged to him and not to the king. He had built it and no one could throw her out of there. This might not sound a very attractive proposition but was the best solution her father could find to the problem. The state was strict about who was allowed to live in a government-owned house. At least she would have some kind of security.

Although marriage was thought to be the ideal state there is no actual evidence for weddings. There is not even an Ancient Egyptian word that means 'to wed'. When a marriage took place the couple seem to have simply moved in together after the prospective bridegroom had gained the consent of the girl's father. The bride would usually play her part in setting up home and bring with her such things as pieces of furniture and textiles to make the house more comfortable and possibly cooking pots and utensils as well. Whatever they were they would be regarded as her own personal property which she was always able to keep even if the marriage ended in divorce. Women could also inherit land and other property and this, too, was always seen as hers. In this way they were much better off than women in Victorian England when everything they owned (even their clothes) technically became their husbands when they married.

That things did not always go smoothly in a marriage is known from several texts such as this record of a court case which tells of a man, Amen-em-ope who was brought before the village court accused of repeatedly beating his wife. The court consisted of the chief workman, Khonsu, the scribes Wen-nefer and Amen-nakhte and the two deputy foremen, Amen-kha and In-her-kau and another officer called Nefer-hotep. Amen-em-ope was found to be guilty. His mother was summoned and he had to swear an oath promising not to do it again.

Another text tells of a young couple who, although married, were still living separately with their parents for some reason that is not explained. Maybe the arrangement was more like an engagement and they were still 'saving up' to furnish their future home. Be that as it may, one day the young man went round to his bride's house only to find that she had been seduced by another of the workmen, Mery-Sakhmet, son of the wealthy draughtsman, Menna. The young man complained to the village officials but because Menna was an influential person in the village they didn't believe the young man and he was punished with one-hundred blows of a stick! Fortunately, he was defended by the chief workman, In-her-kau, who said this had been a grave miscarriage of justice. The chief scribe of the village, Amen-nakhte, then made Mery-Sakhmet swear an oath promising to keep away from the bride – otherwise he would have his ears and nose cut off. However, this did not deter the arrogant Mery-Sakhment and before long he seduced her again. This time he made her pregnant. This was too much even for his father who personally dragged him up before the village officials who made him swear another oath promising not to go near her again and agreeing that if he broke his promise he would have to do forced labour in the quarries at Elephantine.

Sometimes the wife was the guilty one as the letter from another woman to the wife's husband reveals. She reminds him that she has already told him about his wife's promiscuous behaviour and advises him to do something about it.

In happier circumstances as well as owning her personal property, the wife would have a share in the wealth created during the course of the marriage. This was only a third as opposed to two thirds that was the husband's share but the wife was allowed to keep it if her husband died or if he divorced her. If she was responsible for the break-up of the marriage, however, then she had to forfeit her share. Women could also give their property to whoever they wished as is evidenced by wills.

In the Ancient Egyptian Wisdom Texts where the reader is told how to conduct his life, children are exhorted to respect their mother and look after her in her old age just as she cared for them when they were little. Many of the texts show that many children did just that, but others show that some did not. The lady, Naunakhte, had some property of her own and decided in her will to reward her good children but to disinherit those who had neglected her. She had been married twice and when her first husband died she inherited some property from him which was hers to do with as she liked. She had no children by this first marriage but had eight by her second husband. They were the ones about whom her decision was made. The will is dated to Year 3 of Ramesses VI, 4th month of the inundation, day 3 and states that this is a formal declaration before the court deciding to whom she will leave her property. In other words this is her will. She had eight children and decided to share her property with the four of them who had been good to her in her old age while those who had neglected her were to get nothing. She then gives the names of the good children who are to inherit and then those of the neglectful children who were to be disinherited.

The court at Deir el-Medina was used to prosecute women as well as protect their rights. One woman called Heria was accused of stealing one of the workmen's tools. The members of the court interrogated her and asked if she had indeed stolen these tools. She replied that she had not and so she was made to swear an oath to that effect. She took the oath, but the court were not satisfied and sent someone to search her house. They found the missing tool and not only that, but also some ritual vessels she had stolen from the local temple! As Heria was not only guilty of theft, but also of perjury and blasphemy against the gods, she was declared 'worthy of death'. However, we do not know what happened to her in the end as the local court was not allowed to put people to death and she was sent to the vizier's court at Thebes for sentencing and punishment.

Very occasionally women were 'on the bench'. One text is dated to Year 28, third month of winter, day 22. It doesn't say what the case was about but it gives a list of the villagers who were in charge of the court that day. Along with three of the workmen two ladies were mentioned, one is not named but the other was called Meryt-Mut.

In order to obtain justice some people consulted oracles, especially if they were not satisfied with the village court. They used it as a sort of Court of Appeal. At Deir el-Medina this took the form of a procession during which the statue of King Amenhotep I was carried on a ceremonial boat on the shoulders of priests who were chosen from the workmen. Amenhotep I seems to have been the founder of the village and was worshipped as its patron. Anyone could halt the procession and put a question to the oracle. The question had to be one that could be answered with a simple 'yes' or 'no'. Often they were about the rightful ownership of property. If the answer was 'yes' the boat moved forward and if it was 'no' it moved back. One man, Kha-em-weset, asked about a hut that had belonged to his grandfather, Baki, but was now being claimed by the workman Nefer-hotep. Kha-em-weset asked the statue of the king to judge between them. His question was, 'Should Neferhotep be allowed to keep the hut? The god moved backwards very decisively. Just to make sure Kha-em-weset asked again, 'Should it be given to Kha-em-weset?' and the boat moved forward decisively. Kh-em-weset was delighted.

The oracle was once used to find out if a woman had some stolen property. This case was a very delicate one because the woman accused was the daughter of a very important man, the Scribe of the Village, Amen-nakhte, and the man who accused her only a lowly chisel-bearer. He claimed she had stolen two garments. The best way of getting round this tricky situation was to consult the oracle rather than take her to court. The procession went round the village, stopping at all the houses. When they got to the house of Amen-nakhte the god agreed (the boat moved forward) saying, 'They are with his daughter'. The question was asked again and again the boat moved forward. There was really no arguing with that. So Amen-Nakhte was shamed in front of the whole gang of workers by having to admit that it was his daughter who had stolen them.

The women of the village had little opportunity to earn an income. Their main job was to look after the house and care for the family which was generally not very large. A village census shows that families were relatively small. Only one house had as many as five people living there although the elderly who could no longer work sometimes also had to be accommodated. The most common way of earning a little extra was by weaving or sewing. One lady wrote to her sister saying, *'Please be quick about weaving me that shawl. I want to wear it at the festival. Otherwise I haven't a thing to wear!'*

Another woman wrote to her friend asking her to give her a tunic and to go and harvest some vegetables she owed her. This note implies that she had already provided her friend with some service or goods earlier and was now being paid for whatever it had been.

Very few people could read and write in Ancient Egypt so it is very unusual to see women sending notes to one another. Their husbands, however, were literate. They were artists and to get to be an artist they would have had to be trained as a scribe. In any case it was necessary for them to be literate. Much of the decoration of the royal tombs was in the form of spells and prayers to enable the king to reach Osiris, God of the Dead, and to enjoy his afterlife. So the texts had to be correct in order for the spells to work. Some of the men's ability seems to have rubbed off onto their wives as there is no evidence for women in the village having any formal education.

Although women, generally speaking, were not allowed to work in the administration they often took responsibility for their husband's affairs when he was away from home. A good example of this is this letter from a woman named Henut-tawy to her husband the village scribe, Nesy-su-amen-em-ope. He had left the village for a few days to collect grain for the workmen's wages. While he was away his wife was responsible for the supervision of the grain he was sending to the village stores. His wife writes to him to keep him in the picture and tells him that she strongly suspects the suppliers have brought less than the agreed amount. After a long formal greeting she writes that he told her to expect eighty sacks of grain from the fisherman who was transporting them. When she went to collect them he only gave her seventy-two-and-a-half sacks. When she complained the fisherman and his companions had apparently paid themselves two-and-a-half sacks each. Henut-tawy was very worried about this especially as an army officer had been sent to take the grain away to the storerooms at the temple of Medinet Habu. She ends by asking her husband to come home as quickly as possible as the vizier (the top official in the land) has written with instructions about distributing the grain to the workers.

Childbirth was a very important part of a woman's life. In the days of little medical knowledge it was often a very dangerous procedure and prayers were often offered to Hathor, goddess of fertility and sexual love for her help in conceiving a child and protection of the mother in childbirth. Walls of houses were sometimes decorated with images of Hathor or Bes, also a protector of the family. In the reception area of the houses at Deir el-Medina are mud brick benches which are sometimes called 'birthing beds' but their use is not really certain because women seem to have given birth in a crouching position. The hieroglyph for birth shows a crouching woman with the head and arms of a baby emerging from between her legs. Some pottery fragments from Deir el-Medina show a woman nursing her baby in a little booth made of leafy branches which may have been placed on the roof to separate the mother from the rest of the family.

The main problem with all of this is that it comes from only one village where the men and some of the women were literate and could write notes and letters to each other and keep records about many areas of life in their community.

Deir el-Medina was a very special place. It is not true to say that it was a village where 'ordinary' people lived. This was a community of very skilled and gifted craftsmen and their wives. Most ordinary people lived in villages where the majority would have been occupied in farming the land and were not able to read and write. The sort of evidence we find at Deir el-Medina is not available from anywhere else so we do not know whether the information which comes from Deir el-Medina applies to other places elsewhere in Ancient Egypt.

Chapter 5

Hatshepsut – the female pharaoh

Hatshepsut was a very capable woman who lived in the 15th century BC. She was the daughter of one pharaoh, the wife of another and later became a pharaoh herself, and a very successful one at that. While she was married to Thutmose II she was a queen, but after his death she became first, regent on behalf of her six-year-old stepson, Thutmose III, and after some years, king and ruled with him for fourteen years before she disappears from history. 'Queen' in Ancient Egypt meant 'wife of a king' and queens did not normally rule as our Queen Elizabeth does, so she called herself 'King' and on her monuments she is dressed like a king and wears the king's crown and not the vulture headdress that queens wore and Hatshepsut herself wore when she was the wife of Thutmose II. This does not mean that she actually went round bare-chested and wearing the royal kilt. She is simply making the point on her monuments that she is a king and not a queen.

This was a very important distinction. Kings in Ancient Egypt were considered to be gods. They had five names altogether. One of these was his Horus name and another went with his title Son of Re (the sun god). Another title was 'King of the Two Lands'. All of these were references to mythology and demonstrated the king's divine origins.

In the *Myth of Kingship* the god Osiris was originally a real king of Egypt. He taught his people how to farm the land and to worship the gods. He was so popular that his wicked brother, Seth, decided to kill him and take the throne himself. After sneakily taking Osiris' measurements he invited him to a party where he offered to give a beautifully carved box to anyone who could fit into it exactly. No prizes for guessing who did! Seth then slammed down the lid and threw the box, with the body of Osiris in it, into the Nile.

It drifted out into the Mediterranean Sea and ended up at Byblos on the coast of modern Lebanon. It came to rest against a magic tree which grew round it at a rapid rate. One day the king came down to the seashore and saw what was now a massive tree and had it cut down to use as a column to support the ceiling in his palace. Soon after this along came Isis, the sister and wife of Osiris, desperately looking for the body of her husband. She had magic powers and soon realised that it was inside the box inside the tree that was now in the palace. Isis went to the palace and got a job as nursemaid to the king's baby son. The queen looked into the nursery one night to check on the baby and to her horror she saw Isis putting her little son in and out of a fire. She let out an ear-splitting shriek and dismissed Isis on the spot. Isis then told her that she was a goddess and that she had been purifying him. She added that the queen had just ruined her son's chances of becoming immortal. (Don't try this at home!)

Before she left, Isis begged the tree with the body of her husband inside and went off back to Egypt. When she got as far as the Delta she was tired and fell asleep. Unfortunately Seth was prowling around and when he found the body of Osiris he hacked it into fourteen pieces to make sure he was really dead this time and then scattered the pieces all over Egypt. Isis was heart-broken when she discovered what had happened but immediately enlisted the help of their sister, Nephthys, and together they went round the entire land picking up the pieces. Isis and Nephthys then changed themselves into kites (birds of prey). They reassembled the body, then flapped their wings to create air which Osiris breathed and so was able to come alive again.

However, the Egyptians now had a problem. They decided that even though Osiris had come back to life he could not be a king of the Living anymore and instead he went to the Underworld to be king of the Dead. So who was going to be King of Egypt now? Osiris had a son and heir, Horus, and many people thought he should be king next, but his brother, Seth, thought he had a better right to the throne. They quarrelled fiercely about it and eventually took the matter to the Divine Court. At first the gods thought the best solution would be to divide Egypt between them, Horus having the throne of the North and Seth that of the South. Then Geb, the earth god and president of the court, overturned the decision and gave both Lands to Horus. All the future kings of Egypt considered themselves to be a reincarnation of Horus and to be King of the Two Lands. Although it sounds an unlikely story it was taken very seriously by the Egyptians and explains why Hatshepsut had to insist she was king with the god-given right to rule and not a queen.

In the past Hatshepsut was cast as 'an unscrupulous, scheming woman', exceedingly ambitious, even power-crazy, determined to have the young Thutmose III under her thumb and be the real ruler of the land. She was also said to have had a long-standing love affair with one of her officials, Senenmut. Later on, Thutmose became so fed up with Hatshepsut's overbearing ways that he had her murdered. All of this would have made a very good novel but, unfortunately for the perpetrators of these ideas, none of this seems to have been true.

The real story is even more remarkable if not quite as juicy. In Ancient Egypt the king was thought to be chosen by the gods who gave him the authority to rule. However, this did not stop some people from trying to get rid of the king and take the throne either for themselves or a relative. The kings usually had more than one wife and there are two examples of harem conspiracies in Egyptian history where a lesser queen has tried to dethrone the reigning king and make her son ruler instead. Another king, Amenemhet I, is thought to have been a usurper and was later assassinated himself.

King Thutmosis III had a very long reign of fifty-four years so he must have been very young when his father died and he became king. There may have been several people who would have entertained the idea of doing away with the young boy and taking the throne themselves, so it is quite likely that Hatshepsut decided to be regent to protect the rights of her stepson.

It is more difficult to explain why, instead of resigning this position after about six years when the young king would have been considered old enough to rule alone, she made herself joint king with Thutmose III. Maybe she felt he still needed her support and in any case she was just doing what many kings in the past had done. From the Middle Kingdom onwards some of the kings reigned alone for a number of years and then co-opted their son to rule with them. The practice started with Amenemhet, the first king of Dynasty Twelve. Egyptian sources suggest that he may have been the same person as the vizier Amenemhet mentioned in the rock stela of King Mentuhotep IV. He was sent on an expedition accompanied by ten-thousand soldiers to procure a piece of stone to make the king's coffin lid. He would therefore have had the opportunity to mount a revolution and does not seem to have been related to Mentuhotep's family, so may well have usurped the throne. Having seen how easily this could be done he decided to co-opt his son, Senusret, as joint ruler so that on his death the succession would go smoothly, the new king having already been accepted as king when he reigned together with his father. Be that as it may, this was the practice for all the kings of that Dynasty so Hatshepsut wasn't doing anything startlingly new.

In her funerary temple at Deir el-Bahri Hatshepsut emphasised her right to be king by including the story of her divine birth in the decoration. When the story opens the god Amun-Re, the sun god, seems to be speaking to the Council of the Gods. He prophesies the birth of Hatshepsut and her subsequent rise to power. Her mother, Queen Ahmose is then chosen as the mother of the child of Amun-Re, that is Hapshetsut, who is going to be the next king.

In the next scene Amun-Re, cunningly disguised as the queen's husband, Thutmose I, visits Ahmose in the night and impregnates her. The queen wakes up and recognises Amun-Re by the beautiful fragrance which has flooded the palace. He tells her that she will have his baby daughter, who will be called Hatshepsut and be king of the whole land.

Amun-Re then speaks to Khnum, one of the creator gods and tells him to go and '*make her together with her ka…fashion her better than all the gods, shape for me this daughter whom I have begotten*'. Khnum is shown as a potter; he agrees and forms Hatshepsut and her 'ka' (her double) on his potter's wheel.

After this, Queen Ahmose is led into the birth room. Hatshepsut is born and is given to some of the goddesses to nurse. The wise god, Thoth, announces the news to Amun-Re and so Hatshepsut assumes the title Son of Re which is one of the five titles of all Ancient Egyptian kings.

To make doubly sure that she has made herself absolutely clear, Hatshepsut then claims that her earthly father then summoned the court and presented his daughter to them. He said,

This is my daughter, Hatshepsut. I have appointed her…She is my successor upon my throne…She shall command my people in every place in my palace…she will lead you. He who pays her homage will live; he who speaks evil against her shall die. All you officials of my court, the nobles and chiefs of the people take note!

They all agreed and kissed the ground at his feet. They proclaimed Hatshepsut as King and on New Year's Day they held her coronation.

None of this was true but it was a good piece of royal propaganda designed to dispel any doubts about the legitimacy of her right to rule. If the chief of the gods had commanded she should be the next king and her father had ordered the court to accept her as sovereign, who could argue with that?

There is a small chapel dedicated to the goddess Hathor attached to Hatshepsut's funerary temple at Deir el-Bahri. Hathor was one of the mythological mothers of kings. (Yes you could have more than one mother!) Sometimes she is shown as a cow and sometimes as a beautiful lady with a cow's ears. In this chapel Hathor is shown as a cow licking the child Hatshepsut just as a cow licks her calf. So here we have another powerful piece of royal propaganda.

Back in the main temple there is a series of beautiful carved and painted scenes depicting an expedition sent to the mysterious and exotic land of Punt. One of the main activities of kings was to send expeditions to far-flung places to obtain luxury goods both for themselves but also to reward their officials and army commanders for faithful service. It is still not quite certain where Punt was. It seems to have been either somewhere along the Red Sea coast or on the Horn of Africa. The scenes show Hatshepsut's expedition arriving in Punt accompanied by a large army. The people of Punt lived in beehive-shaped houses built on platforms supported by stilts presumably to keep them safe from attack by wild animals. They kept cattle and grew myrrh trees from which they obtained incense. The Egyptians used incense in their temple rituals and Hatshepsut says that the main purpose of the expedition was to obtain incense for use in the worship of 'her father', Amun. The King and Queen of Punt met the expedition members on their arrival and goods were exchanged. There was no money at this time so they 'bought' goods by offering the King and Queen goods of equal value to the ones they wanted from Punt. As well as incense Hatshepsut also wanted large quantities of gold. She tried to give the impression that the Egyptians had forced the people of Punt to give them these goods as tribute from a conquered people but really they were trading. In the captions that tell you what is going on in the various scenes the gold is called 'tribute' but there is also a list of the goods that the Egyptians had brought with them as payment – *bread, beer, wine, meat, fruit, everything found in Egypt, according to the command of the court.*

Another section shows the homeward journey. The ships heavily loaded with *all the marvels of the country of Punt, all goodly fragrant woods, heaps of myrrh resin, myrrh trees, gold, ebony and ivory, eye paint, panther skins and live animals.*

The scene shows monkeys scampering about in the rigging of the ships and the text says they brought back some of the people too. No wonder Hatshepsut claimed no expedition had ever been so successful before. She blows her own trumpet in this way to make sure people realise she had made a good job of this aspect of being a king.

Another side of being a king was to pay great respect to the gods by building temples and taking part in rituals and festivals. Another series of painted reliefs at Deir el-Bahri show her taking part in the New Year Festival and there are many instances of her building or restoring temples all over Egypt, some of them in conjunction with Thutmose III. In the temple of Karnak there is a boat shrine of Hatshepsut. This was where the sacred boat of Amun was kept for most of the year. At the New Year festival it carried the statue of Amun-Re in its shrine along the river to Luxor where he spent several days with his wife, the goddess Mut. The shrine is partly decorated with scenes showing both Hatshepsut and Thutmose taking part in this festival and worshipping the sacred boat as it sails along the Nile.

Here the two kings are acting in harmony and there is no evidence that they were hostile to each other in other spheres. Thutmose III appears to have spent the early part of his reign engaged in military training and there is evidence for some foreign campaigns at this time in which Hatshepsut was also engaged.

Nothing more is heard of Hatshepsut after Year 21 of the reign of Thutmose. In Year 22 he set out on a great campaign in Syria-Palestine and won an important victory when he defeated a coalition of many of the petty rulers of the area. In his account of the battle of Megiddo he said that the capture of Megiddo was the capture of a thousand towns! This seems to make nonsense of the story that Thutmose murdered Hatshepsut. If he could be so successful in the very first year of his sole rule, he must have been pretty powerful before. So maybe by this time they decided that Thutmose no longer needed the support of Hatshepsut or maybe she felt that after twenty-one years of protecting his interests she would like to retire. She would have been about forty years old by then and quite an old lady by the standards of the time. People had much shorter lives than is usual today so maybe she just died. There is no reason to think she was murdered. If Thutmose III had really hated her so much that he wanted to kill her, why wait twenty-one years to do so?

Nonetheless after her disappearance the name of Hatshepsut was removed on many of her monuments and replaced by that of her husband, Thutmose II. Who did this and why? It used to be thought that this was another example of the antagonism of Thutmose III. However, there is no evidence that clearly states when the defacements took place. It need not have been the work of Thutmose at all, but of a later king who disapproved of her. Moreover, Thutmose finished some of her monuments on her behalf after her disappearance. The real answer seems to lie in the Ancient Egyptian concept of what was right and proper. They believed in something called *ma'at*. It is not possible to translate this with one word in English. It means a great many things, for example: truth, what is right, and justice. Generally speaking it was the idea of the correct way to conduct your life, the way in which the god, Re, had ordained that the universe should run. Having a woman on the throne did not fit in with this idea.

A later king, Seti I, put up a list of kings in his temple at Abydos. Abydos had always been a very important place connected with the kings of Egypt. The list was supposed to contain all the kings from the very beginning of Egyptian history down to Seti I. Ramesses II put up a similar list in his temple nearby. However, these lists were not complete. They only included the names of kings that Seti and Ramesses approved of. They themselves were not descended from earlier kings but were army commanders who took over when there were no true heirs to the throne. So it was extra important for them to present themselves as True Kings, especially as they were not. They did this by adding their names to the list of what they considered to be true Horuses and leaving out those they thought weren't. So they missed out the kings of Intermediate Periods when the kingship was disputed and when there were several 'kings' at one time. The divinely approved system was when there was one King of the Two Lands as in the conclusion of the story of Horus and Seth. King Akhenaten was not liked by many people because he upset them by discarding some of the old religious beliefs, so they left him off too.

There were no women whatsoever on these lists even though it was known there had been at least three other queens who had ruled as kings. They had ruled only briefly at the end of dynasties when there was no one else to take the throne. They seem to have been regarded as A Bad Thing having ruled without divine approval. Even though Hatshepsut had spent a long time in office and had ruled competently and well they dismissed her on the grounds that a woman on the throne did not fit their concept of *ma'at*, of what was right and proper in the eyes of the gods. That idea and not the hatred of Thutmose seems to have been the reason for the erasure of her name on monuments and her exclusion from the king lists.

And what about Senenmut? Was he really her lover? We shall probably never know. He was certainly a highly trusted official and became tutor to her little daughter, Neferrure. He was also in charge of some of her building works. When he died he was buried in a tomb very close to that of Hatshepsut. This would indicate that they were very close friends, perhaps, but doesn't make them lovers. However, there appear to have been rumours of something of the sort as in one old tomb near Deir el-Bahri that had been used as a workmen's hut, there is a very suggestive sketch of a couple, one wearing the king's crown and the other a workman's cap. So there may be something in it after all.

Chapter 6

The God's Wife of Amun

Women in Ancient Egypt played little part in public life. However, from the Old Kingdom onwards, the wives of officials often had roles as musicians and singers in the cult of the goddess Hathor. At Deir el-Medina much of the music which accompanied religious events was provided by the women of the village. They are shown in tomb paintings singing and dancing and holding Hathor's sacred instruments, the *sistrum* and *menat*. The *sistrum* was a type of musical rattle usually made of metal and decorated with a head of Hathor and a *menat* was a many-stringed necklace composed of strands of metal beads. They were shaken in front of the statue of the goddess during rituals held in her honour. Queens and princesses are sometimes shown using them too.

One very important position that royal women could hold was that of God's Wife of Amun. From the Middle Kingdom onwards the cult of Amun became increasingly important. He was closely linked with the sun-god, Re, and by the New Kingdom he was known as Amun-Re and was the chief of the gods, although many others were also worshipped. He was the god, who above all other deities, was said to choose the kings who were regarded as his sons. One of their five titles was Son of Re and was written before the name they were given when they were born.

Hatshepsut made much of this idea when she had her divine birth depicted on the walls of her funerary temple at Deir el-Bahri. As you may remember, the god Amun-Re is shown visiting her mother, impregnating her and announcing that she was to be the mother of the next king – his daughter, Hatshepsut! From the beginning of the New Kingdom some royal women were given the title God's Wife of Amun. Because of the depictions in Hatshepsut's temple and another similar series in the temple at Luxor showing the divine birth of Amenhotep III, it was thought at one time that the queen in question was shown here fulfilling her role as the wife of the god Amun. This led to the theory that all kings of Egypt got their right to rule from their mother as God's Wife. This is now known not to be true. If it were, all the queens of Egypt would have to be descended from their predecessor and they are not. Some were foreigners and others were commoners. In fact, the sons inherited their position as next king from their father, the previous king, as laid down in the Myth of Kingship.

So what was this position of God's Wife of Amun? It was clearly very important to the royal women who held it. Some, like Hatshepsut, who was also God's Wife of Amun when she was the wife of Thutmose II, preferred this title to that of Wife of the King or even Principal Wife of the King. When she became king, however, she could no longer be God's Wife and she gave this position to her daughter, Neferrure. On monuments queens and God's Wives are shown wearing quite different headdresses. Queens wear the vulture headdress but God's Wives have a simple band of gold with ribbons attached. They are depicted offering to Amun while queens are not. They are priestesses rather than queens (that is king's wives) although many of them were both!

Later on, from the reign of Ramesses VI, the God's Wives began to wield political power too. Ramesses VI gave the title to his daughter, Isis. From then on the God's Wife was always the daughter of the king and so had political as well as religious power in Thebes where the main cult centre of Amun was. This was extremely important as at that time the High Priests of Amun were becoming increasingly influential there. They came from the most powerful families in Thebes whose members were often viziers and army commanders. Some High Priests combined these posts and when the Two Lands of Egypt were divided at the end of Dynasty 20 the kings ruled the North and the High Priests controlled the South.

Even later, in Dynasties 25 and 26 when Egypt was again reunited and the kings ruled the whole country it was very useful for them to have a daughter in such an influential position. The Dynasty 25 kings ruled from

Memphis, the traditional capital city (near modern Cairo) and the Dynasty 26 from even further north, from Sais in the Delta. The High Priests were still a force to be reckoned with, however, and the God's Wife was able to curb their power. At this time she was not allowed to marry and have children so she had to adopt the daughter of the next king as heiress to this position. This meant the king could make sure he always had power in Thebes and that other daughters and secondary queens were less able to support rival claimants to the throne and so the succession could proceed more smoothly.

One reason the God's Wife was so influential was because, especially in later times, she was extremely wealthy and owned vast estates of land near Thebes.

Fortunately, a stela (document written on stone) exists which records the adoption of Nitocris, daughter of Psammtik I, first king of Dynasty 26, by Shepenwepet, daughter of Taharqa, the most famous king of Dynasty 25. It also records the transfer of all the property of Shepenwepet to Nitocris. The purpose of the document was to legalise the transfer of the wealth and position of God's Wife to the new dynasty and so enable it to gain control of Thebes. The document describes her triumphal procession to Thebes:

In Year 9 first month of the first season, day 28 Nitocris left the palace dressed in fine linen and beautifully made up with green eye paint. She was accompanied by a great procession of her servants and palace officials who cleared the way for her as she went down to the harbour to take ship for Thebes. A huge flotilla sailed south with her, the vessels laden with treasures from the king's palace and commanded by the most important officers in the land.

When she arrived in Thebes she was greeted by an enormous crowd who warmly welcomed her. Then she met Shepenwepet who greeted her affectionately and formally transferred to Nitocris all her property. The transaction was put into writing and witnessed by the prophets, priests and all the staff of the temple of Amun at Thebes.

Then follows a long list of the property concerned including numerous estates throughout Egypt and all the goods produced on them as a major source of her income. Huge amounts were also donated by the powerful Fourth Prophet of Amun, Montuemhet, his son and his wife as offerings on Nitocris' behalf to the temple of Amun in Thebes. These included daily deliveries of bread, wine and beer, vegetables and cakes and monthly donations of oxen and geese. All of this was to be given in perpetuity – *abiding, abiding, conveyed, conveyed, imperishable and ineffaceable, for ever and ever, for ever and ever.*

Another interesting inscription written on the statue of Ibe one of the dignitaries in attendance on Nitocris describes her installation ceremony which seems to have been a very grand affair. All the correct rituals were carried out amid great rejoicing and the event was as much like a coronation as anything. Nitocris was carried to the ceremony *in a palanquin borne on poles newly made of silver and gold and inlaid with every precious stone and ordered offerings to be made…*

Ibe also says he later helped Nitocris with her paperwork, supervised the running of her estates and when her palace was in need of repair he was put in charge of the restorations.

Just as Nitocris herself had been adopted by Shepenwepet as the future God's Wife of Amun, so Nitocris in her turn appointed her successor. She was Ankhesneferibre, daughter of Psammtik II. A second Adoption Stela records the event:

Year 1, third month of summer, day 29, during the reign of Psammtik (II) the king's daughter, Ankhesneferibre, arrived in Thebes. Her 'mother', the God's Wife, Nitocris, came to meet her and they went together to the temple of Amun where Ankhesneferibre was adopted as the future God's Wife.

Three years later Nitocris died and twelve days afterwards Ankhesneferibre went to the temple of Amun where she was installed as God's Wife as had been arranged previously. All the priests and other important people of the land were present and all the proper ceremonies carried out:

There were performed for her all the customary ceremonies for the induction of the God's Wife of Amun by the divine scribe and nine priests of the temple of

Amun. She fastened on all the amulets and ornaments of the God's Wife, and was crowned with a diadem and two plumes to be queen of every circuit of the sun (in the sense that she was wife of Amun who was king of all the gods).

Women in Ancient Egypt were respected socially and legally. They are shown in tomb paintings as equal with men in many ways. Peasant women work in the fields alongside men and upper-class women are seen sitting with men at feasts and parties. As we have seen women could own property and dispose of it as they wished in wills, they could carry on business on their own account and on behalf of their husbands and take people to court.

As women frequently took part in religious events as priestesses, singers and musicians it is perhaps not too surprising that a woman could hold the position of God's Wife of Amun. However, generally speaking, a woman could not hold an official position. In order to become an official in the administration and help run the country they would have had to be trained as a scribe and as there does not seem to have been any official education available for women, they were excluded from government posts.

Women were also barred from the office of king by the Myth of Kingship which has no room for them as rulers. Isis had an important part to play in the myth but only as the wife of Osiris and the mother of Horus. Those women like Hatshepsut who did manage to become rulers were only able to do so by projecting themselves as a king. The position of God's Wife was the only one where a woman could officially wield power, hence the importance of the women who held it.

GREECE

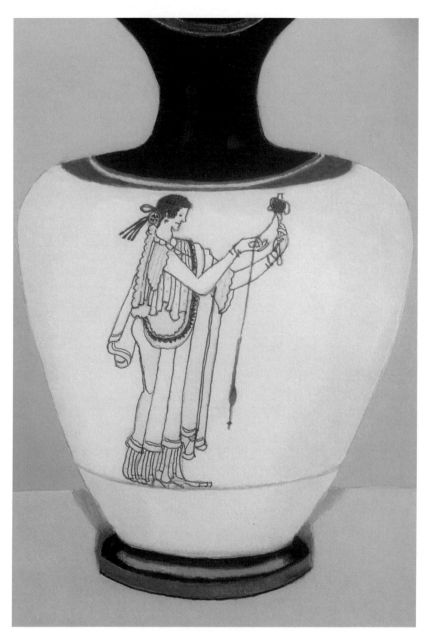

A Greek housewife spinning.

From an Athenian vase (c. 490 BC).

Chapter 7

Women of Ancient Greece

Until comparatively recently Greece was not a united country, but rather a collection of independent city states, loosely connected by a common culture, but often at war with one another. In the fifth and fourth century BC Athens and Sparta were two of the most important city states. The life of women in these states was vastly different. Even within any one particular state women of different social classes were involved in varying activities.

Xenophon, the fifth/fourth century BC Greek writer lived in both Athens and Sparta at various times in his life. In his book the *Oeconomicus,* which is mainly about estate management, he also talks about the importance of family life and the role of women. Their main job, he says, is to manage the household well and their chief purpose in life is to have children and bring them up according to a strict moral code. He also advised Greek men to marry young healthy women who could be trained to become good wives! Women were expected to contribute to the household economy by spinning and weaving and making clothes. Generally speaking they lived secluded lives and were not allowed to own property and dispose of it as they liked.

Sources of information about them are scenes on Greek vases. A red-figure vase now in Harvard University shows an idyllic domestic scene. A woman hands her baby to a maidservant while a young man (the eldest son?) looks on. Behind the maid there is a loom. This vase was found in a tomb, which may have belonged to the young wife herself and depicts her as a model wife, or possibly it belonged to her husband and shows the well-run family home he has left behind.

Many vases show a woman spinning and the distaff was a symbol of the model housewife. One vase also has an inscription which says *she is industrious.* One of the best vases is a perfectly preserved jug in the British Museum. It shows a woman spinning and illustrates the technique to perfection. She holds the distaff in her left hand and with her right she holds the thread between her index finger and thumb while the spindle whirls away below. You can also see the hook to which the thread is attached at the top of the spindle and the weight at the bottom which keeps the thread taut. The scene is painted on a white background. This is very unusual and means that this vase is rather special, probably a gift. It could have been a wedding present and the design a model of wifely virtue for her to follow. The jug shape is also probably significant. At religious ceremonies it was the woman who poured the wine from such a jug into a bowl held by her husband who then poured it onto the ground as a libation (liquid offering).

A further scene on some Greek vases show a group of women going to fetch water from the fountain house. This scene raises lots of questions. Who were these women? 'Nice' women did not often go out and would never be seen at the fountain house which seems to have been a very noisy and unsavoury place. However, the women depicted here all appear to be well dressed so are probably not slaves whose job this would normally have been. One such vase in the British Museum also shows the gods Dionysos and Hermes present, so are we looking at a festival here in which water was poured out as this would have made the presence of women respectable?

Some women in Ancient Greece were priestesses. They can be recognised on Greek vases and stelas (grave markers) by the large temple keys they hold. This shows their role was to lock and unlock the temple doors. As the temples often contained large amounts of gold and silver this was a very responsible job. The most important priestess in Athens served Athena Polias, the patron goddess who protected the city. Married women could take this position which was passed down in families and held for life. One famous priestess of Athena Polias was called Lysimache. She held the position for sity-four years and lived to the ripe old age of eighty-eight.

One of the priestesses of Athena Polias can be seen on the Parthenon Frieze in the British Museum where she is taking part in the Festival of the

Panathenaia when the goddess was presented with a new robe. This festival was held annually and on a very grand scale every four years. It was held on what was supposed to be Athena's birthday and included a procession of young girls carrying ritual vessels, young men leading the sacrificial animals, chariots and charioteers, and the cavalry. The robe or *peplos* as it was called was hoisted as a sail on the mast of a boat on wheels and was then offered to Athena.

Some women had some basic education and knew something about how the state was run. To be a citizen of Athens you had to be a free-born male. You would then be allowed to take part in the day-to-day running of the city and in the discussion of important issues like the rebuilding of the Parthenon (the temple of the goddess Athena) after the Persian Wars, and going to war. Slaves and women could not be citizens. However, because women had no political rights that does not mean they had no influence on politics. Aristophanes, one of the famous Athenian playwrights of the fifth century BC wrote extremely funny plays about it. One was about an Athenian woman called Lysistrata. She was appalled by the Peloponnesian War which had been going on and on for years and was devastating Greece. Many men had been killed leaving widows and bereaved mothers behind not to mention the young women who would never get married because there were no men left to marry. This was a serious problem as at that time unmarried women had no place in society. This war was mainly between Athens and Sparta but the whole of Greece was involved because all the states took sides and supported one or other of them. They often complicated matters by changing sides.

When the play opens Lysistrata is waiting for women from all over Greece to come to a meeting she has called to put before them her plan to end the war. When her neighbour comes out Lysistrata complains that the others are slow in appearing. Calonice, her neighbour, says that it is very difficult for women to get out of the house as they have to look after their husbands, wake up the slaves and feed and wash the baby and get it to sleep. Aristophanes is having a dig at a woman's role in Ancient Greece here. Lysistrata replies angrily that what she has to say is much more important than any of that. She wants them to unite together to save Greece. Calonice replies,

And how are we going to do that? How can we possibly achieve anything so grand or noble? All we ever do is sit around at home looking pretty wearing see-through dresses and sexy make-up.

Lysistrata says she is going to use exactly these weapons to save Greece. When the others come she explains that she wants them all to tease their husbands by making themselves look very attractive and desirable and then refuse to sleep with them. In the end the men are so fed up they agree to make peace. Unfortunately, this was only what happened in the play. In reality the war continued until Athens was finally defeated and utterly exhausted. Many opportunities to make peace had been turned down by politicians thinking only of themselves and their personal power. Greece never really recovered from this disaster. If only they had listened to Aristophanes!

Another of his plays was called *Women in the Assembly* and has the women of Athens taking over the running of the city. The leader of the women is Praxagora. She calls them all together to see they are all ready for action. They have to go to the Assembly (the Athenian parliament) disguised as men. One woman says:

I have grown an absolute forest under my arms as per instructions. And every day, as soon as my husband went out, I oiled myself all over and stood in the sun all day to get brown.

Another said almost the same having done all she could to make herself look like a man and not a bit like a woman at all. Then Praxagora asked them if they had all brought the false beards like she had told them to. They all had and she could see they had done everything else they had agreed, having pinched their husbands' shoes, walking sticks and cloaks while they were still asleep. They then had to hurry to put on their disguises and go to the Assembly in time to get the best seats near the speaker's platform. Once there they practised their speeches. Some of the women were hopeless. One of them even began by addressing the Assembly as 'Ladies' while others swore by the goddesses Aphrodite and Persephone which no man would ever have done.

Praxagora, however, was spot on. She addressed them so:

Gentlemen, my interest in the welfare of this state is no less than yours, but I deeply deplore the way in which its affairs are being handled. The task of speaking for the people is invariably given to crooks and rascals. For every day they spend doing good they spend another ten in doing irreparable harm.

If you try somebody new he turns out to be even worse than the one before. When we were debating the Anti-Spartan Treaty Organization everyone was for it but when it was actually set up everyone was against it and the man who had proposed it was hounded out of the city. Someone proposes new ships for the navy: the poor say yes but the rich men and the farmers say no. One minute you vote to make peace but when the chance to do that arises, you are suddenly against it and the opportunity is lost... However, I have a solution to your problems. I propose we hand over the running of the state to the women. After all they are the ones who run our homes so efficiently.

When Praxagora later made her speech in the Assembly all her disguised supporters voted enthusiastically for her. They were in the majority and so her proposal was passed. The women went on to make the new laws. Everyone was to have an equal share in everything and live on that. There would be no more rich and poor, no more people with huge farms and others with hardly any land at all; no one would have dozens of slaves and others with none at all. There was to be a common stock of all the necessities of life for everybody to share equally. It would be paid for by everybody pooling all their wealth. When the husbands wanted to know how they would persuade people to do this, Praxagora pointed out that there wouldn't be any point in hanging on to your wealth if everything you needed you could get for free!

None of this actually happened at the time and it wasn't until last century that women even got the vote. However, the Greek philosopher, Plato, a few years after the play was written, used some of the ideas in it as the basis for his picture of the ideal state in his book *The Republic*.

Poor women had to go out to work, although there were very few options open to them. Some would do spinning for pay, some could hire themselves out as a wet-nurse, while others sold bread and herbs in the market and garlands for wear at religious ceremonies. Some foreign women became concubines or courtesans if they were educated and provided female company for the men at parties. They were regarded as a class of women in law and were legally protected. Slaves and the poorest women were sometimes forced to become prostitutes. Some of them were flute-girls and other musicians and entertained at rowdy parties.

Although Athenian women had no political rights they did have some legal rights. They could get a divorce and were allowed to give evidence in court. They were not allowed to own property but the State looked after the elderly, orphans and girls who had no brothers so that they were not left destitute if they had no male relative to provide for them.

Spartan women had a much harder life than most Athenian women. Sparta was a state where the emphasis was on physical fitness and military training. Boys from the age of seven were separated from their families and sent to live in barracks where they underwent rigorous discipline. Even Spartan girls had to train hard to make themselves extremely fit. They had always to remember that they were the future mothers of Spartan soldiers and competed against each another in athletic events. This would have been unthinkable in Athens where girls led a secluded life and would certainly not have been allowed to race about and take part in such competitions.

Even Spartan women were not allowed to take part in the Olympic Games even though in the early days of the Games most of the winners came from Sparta. It seems to have been definitely a men-only event, at least in the beginning.

Pausanias, the Greek writer of the second century AD who wrote a guide book to Greece for Roman tourists, is very informative about the Olympic Games and the sights to be seen at Olympia such as the temple of the god Zeus to whom the games were dedicated. He describes a very steep mountain just outside Olympia and says any woman caught trying to get into the Games would be hurled down from the top. However, only one woman was ever caught. She was Kallipateira, a widow who wanted to go to the Games as her son's trainer. So she disguised herself as a man and took her son to Olympia to fight. She was so excited when he won that she jumped over the fence that shut in the trainers and the judges saw that she was a woman. Fortunately for her, they let her off scot-free because her father and brothers and son had all been Olympic winners, but they made a new rule that from then on all trainers had to enter the arena naked.

According to tradition the Olympic Games began in 776 BC and were held every four years until they were stopped by the Roman Emperor Theodosius I in AD 393. They were revived in 1878 by a Frenchman, Baron Pierre de Courbertin and have been held every four years ever since.

At first they were held on just one day and consisted only of running and wrestling. Later more contests were added and spread over five days and eventually included throwing the discus and javelin, boxing, horse racing and chariot races.

One legend about the origins of the Games says they were started by a young prince, Pelops, who fell in love with Hippodameia, daughter of the king of the Greek state of Pisa. Many other young men had also fallen in love with her and wanted to marry her. Her father, King Oenomaus, always set them a very difficult task. He said he would only allow someone to marry her who could beat him in a chariot race. If they lost they would be put to death. Oenomaus had exceptional horses and rode in his speedy chariot clad in special armour given him by Ares, god of war. Needless to say he always won and by the time Pelops arrived on the scene Oenomaus had nailed up a dozen or so heads of the defeated suitors over the door of his palace. Not wanting to suffer the same fate Pelops bribed the king's charioteer to loosen the bronze axle pins in the king's chariot wheels (some say replace them with wax ones) so that when Oenomaus started to drive his chariot the wheels came off and Oenomaus fell out. Pelops claimed his bride and set up the Games in celebration of his victory.

Married women were never allowed to attend the Games, but at some point a special running match was introduced for girls who were virgins. Every four years a select group of sixteen young women was chosen to weave a robe for the goddess Hera, wife of Zeus in mythology, and the same girls held games in her honour. Pausanias writes that they ran with their hair let down and their tunics above their knees with the right breast and shoulder bare. They ran along the Olympic track although not quite so far. The winner got a wreath of olive leaves and a share of the ox they sacrificed to Hera. People say this race also began in antiquity and was started by Hippodameia as a thank offering for her marriage to Pelops.

Part of the decoration on an Athenian wine bowl of the
Late Geometric Period.

It may depict Paris eloping with Helen.

60

Chapter 8

The Women of Troy

In 480 BC the city of Athens had led the Greek states to victory against the Persian Empire. During the war the Persians had destroyed the buildings on the Acropolis at the heart of the city. So after the war the Athenians began to rebuild their city on a grand scale. This was when the Parthenon, the temple to the city goddess, Athena, was built and a great bronze statue of her was put up to celebrate their final victory over the Persians.

Because of her success Athens became rich and powerful. Eventually she became greedy for yet more power and began to build up an empire. Sparta and several other Greek states began to object to her heavy-handed actions and shortly afterwards war broke out again. This war was the Peloponnesian War when the Greek states divided into two leagues headed by Athens and Sparta.

This war dragged on and on and a great many lives were lost on both sides. First one side then the other would win a victory but neither could win the war.

Towards the end of the fifth century BC the Athenian playwright, Euripides, wrote a play called *The Women of Troy* as a protest against the horrors and suffering caused by war. When the play was performed at the Athenian drama festival, the Great Dionysia, in 415 BC, Athens and Sparta had been at war almost continuously for sixteen years with disastrous results. Five times in that period Sparta had invaded the countryside around Athens and destroyed all the crops so that people were dying of hunger. Another time when the country people heard that the Spartans were coming they crowded

61

into the Long Walls, the fortifications which ran from Athens to the sea. Conditions were so overcrowded and unhealthy that there was an outbreak of plague. This caused a great deal of suffering and many people died.

The Greeks had a tradition of a war long ago in the past against the people of Troy (near the west coast of modern Turkey) when the Greeks had completely destroyed that city. The war had begun with a beauty competition. One of the princes of Troy, Paris, had been asked to be judge and decide who was the most beautiful of three goddesses, Hera, in mythology the wife of the chief god, Zeus, Athena, patron goddess of Athens, and Aphrodite, the goddess of love.

The competition took place at the wedding of a mortal man, Peleus, and the goddess, Thetis. All the gods and goddesses had been invited except Eris, the goddess of strife. She went all the same determined to cause trouble in revenge. To get her own back she rolled an apple into the midst of the celebrations. Carved into it were the words *to the fairest*. Paris had to decide who to give it to. The three goddesses all thought it should be them and tried to bribe Paris with gifts. Hera said if he chose her she would give him unlimited power, Athena promised victory in war and Aphrodite said her gift would be the most beautiful woman in the world as his wife. Paris chose Aphrodite but that turned out to be a very unwise choice.

The woman he fell in love with, Helen, was already married to Menelaus, the king of Sparta. Paris had been invited to the palace in Sparta and had been lavishly entertained by the king. You can imagine how furious Menelaus was when he discovered that Paris had broken all the laws of hospitality and run off with his wife. He immediately informed his brother, Agamemnon, king of Mycenae, who also summoned the kings of all the other Greek states. They got together a huge army and a great fleet of ships and sailed off to Troy to get Helen back. However, this was not a simple task and the war dragged on for ten years without the Greeks having achieved success. The city of Troy seemed to be invincible.

At last, Odysseus, the cunning king of Ithaca, thought of a dastardly plan to get inside the walls of Troy. With the help of Athena the Greeks constructed an enormous wooden horse, big enough for several soldiers to hide inside. Then the others sailed away pretending they had given up the struggle. They left behind one of their men, Sinon, as a spy. Next morning the Trojans were amazed to find the Greek army gone and the Wooden Horse outside the walls. They found Sinon tied up like a prisoner and he pretended to be very angry that he had been deserted by the Greeks. He advised them to take the Wooden Horse into the city and persuaded them it would bring them luck. Little did they know their enemies were hidden inside. That night the Trojans celebrated what they thought was victory but afterwards, when they were all asleep, Sinon let the men out of the Wooden Horse and signalled to the Greeks to come back from where they had been hiding on a nearby island. They quickly sailed back to Troy. The men once concealed within the Wooden Horse let them into the city which they then completely destroyed. The rest of the story is about the atrocities the Greeks committed after the destruction of Troy.

The whole story of the Trojan War was written by Homer and is to be found in *The Iliad*. Euripides' play only deals with the horrors of the aftermath of the war and the suffering of the women and children.

The play opens with the queen and princesses of Troy terrified of what might be going to happen to them now that the fighting was over. Euripides describes *the endless cries of captured women assigned by lottery as slaves to various Greeks*. Hecabe, Queen of Troy, is a desperate figure. Her husband is dead, her sons died in the war. Her daughter, Polyxena, has been slaughtered as a sacrifice on the grave of the Greek hero, Achilles, while another daughter, Cassandra, the prophetess of Apollo, in defiance of all respect for the god, was to be taken forcibly by Agamemnon as his concubine. In her grief Hecabe cries:

> *Here near Agamemnon's tent*
> *Prisoner and slave I sit,*
> *In unpitied exile,*
> *Old, my grey hair ravaged*
> *By the knife of mourning.*
> *Come you widowed brides of Trojan fighting men*
> *Weeping mothers, trembling daughters,*
> *Come, weep with me while the smoke goes up from Troy.*

Later, while she is wondering about where she will be taken she continues:

A queen to fall so low!
On what strange, distant shore
Shall I to whom my country gave
Honour, authority, imperial sway
Be set by some Greek lord
To tend his children or to keep
Watch by his door
An aged, useless ghost, unknown, ignored
A shadow of death – a slave!

When she is told she is to be assigned to Odysseus whom she calls a monster of *wickedness whose tongue…twists truth to lies, friendship to hate, mocks right and honours wrong* she feels this is the last straw, but there is worse to come, Her daughter goes out of her mind with grief and comes to her mother singing a dreadful song of hate and revenge:

Mother, wreath a triumphal garland round my head.
I am to be married to a king: rejoice in it!
If you find me unwilling, take me, make me go!
As sure as Apollo is a prophet, Agammemnon
Shall find me a more fatal bride
Than Helen. I shall kill him and destroy his house
In vengeance for my brothers' and my father's death.

Later in the play, just as we think nothing worse can happen, Euripides describes the fate of Hecabe's daughter-in-law, Andromache, and her little son, Astyages. Andromache is to be the wife of Achilles son. As she says, she is to be a slave in the very family of the man who killed her husband, Hector.

Moreover she sees a messenger coming. When he tells her he has bad news she thinks he means that she and her son are to be separated and go to different masters, but the truth is unimaginably worse. The messenger tells her that such a great man's son cannot be allowed to live and that the Greeks have decided to kill the little boy. He is to be thrown to his death from the battlements of Troy. The words that Andromache utters on hearing this are some of the most heart-breaking in the whole of literature.

O darling child, prized at too great a worth to live!
You die at an enemy's hands and leave me desolate.
Your noble father's greatness which to other men
Brought life and hope will cost you your death…

> *… Little one*

You are crying. Do you understand? You tug my dress,
Cling to my fingers, nestling like a bird under
His mother's wing…

> *…Dear child so young in my arms,*

So precious! O the sweet smell of your skin! When you
Were newly born I wrapped you up, gave you my breast,
Tended you day and night, worn out with weariness –
For nothing, all for nothing! Say goodbye to me
Once more for the last time of all. Come close to me,
Wind your arms around my neck and put your lips to mine.

Greeks! What has he done? Why will you kill this child?

Astyanax was indeed thrown from the battlements and afterwards the messenger came back bearing the little body on his father's shield. He gave the body to Hecabe, Astyanax's grandmother, and told her to prepare it for burial and to use the shield as his coffin. Although she was glad the child was to be given a decent burial, Hecabe was very scathing in her comments.

Bring the rounded shield of Hector; lay it here –
A sign that should be welcome, but now stabs my eyes.
You Greeks are fine fighters, but where is your pride?

Were you so afraid of him that you had to invent
A new death for him?
Poor little head, your soft curls were a garden where your mother planted kisses;
O how cruelly
They were shorn by your city's battlements.
Now through the shattered skull the blood smiles tempting me to unseemly words.
Your little hands — how like your father's.
But when I lift them they hang limp. Dear lifeless lips,
You made me a promise once, nestled against my dress:
'Grandma, when you die,' you said, 'I will cut off
A long curl of my hair for you and bring my friends
With me to grace your tomb with gifts and holy words.'
You broke your promise, Son: Instead I bury you.
                    …What would a poet write for you
As epitaph? 'This child the Argives (Greeks) killed because
They were afraid of him'? An inscription to make all Greece blush!

In this play Euripides is not saying that the Greeks were any worse than anyone else when it came to war. He is simply using the Trojan War as an example to show the horrors of war and demonstrate the suffering, particularly of women and children. We can see plenty of other examples in our own times whenever we turn on the television. Nonetheless, the people of Athens didn't like *The Women of Troy* and Euripides didn't win the drama competition.

Chapter 9

The story of Medea

Medea was a witch. She lived in Colchis, a city of Asia Minor which we call Turkey today. Her father was Aetes and he owned the famous Golden Fleece. One day a stranger arrived in Colchis, a handsome young man named Jason. He was a prince, son of Aeson, the legitimate king of Iolcos in Northern Greece, but who had been usurped by his half-brother, Pelias.

When he was grown-up Jason made up his mind to win the kingdom back, so off he went to Iolcos. On the way he came to a fast flowing river where an old woman was waiting anxiously on the bank. 'Oh dear,' she said as Jason came up to her, 'just look at that water. However am I going to get across?' 'Don't worry,' said Jason, 'I will carry you over,' and with that he picked her up and started to cross. However, when he was only halfway over he began to struggle.

The old woman seemed much heavier than he had thought and he began to wonder whether he would make it. To make matters worse he lost one of his sandals and was very thankful when he reached the other side. As soon as he set her down she vanished into thin air. Jason then realised it was not really an old woman he had been carrying, but the queen of the gods, the goddess Hera.

After praying to Hera to help him, Jason went straight to the palace and asked to see Pelias who was now king. 'I have come to claim my throne,' announced Jason, 'the one you wrongfully took from my father'. Pelias turned rather pale at this, especially as he noticed at once that Jason had lost one of his sandals and an oracle had foretold that he would lose his throne to a young man wearing only one sandal. Many of those present admired Jason for his courage and were glad to see the son of their old king standing up for his rights. Pelias was rather uneasy as he was clearly in the wrong. 'Well,' he said slowly, 'even if you are who you say you are you must prove your worthiness to rule by performing some brave deed. You must go to Colchis and fetch the Golden Fleece.'

An expedition was made ready. The craftsman, Argos, built a magic boat named the *Argo* after him. Fifty-three young men and one woman, Atalanta, the famous runner and huntress, joined Jason and soon they were sailing eagerly across the sea to fulfil their mission.

After many adventures they reached Colchis and went to see King Aetes. 'So you have come to collect the Golden Fleece,' he said grimly. 'Not an easy task I must point out, but if you are determined this is what you must do. Tomorrow at dawn you must yoke bulls to the plough, plough a field and sow it with dragons' teeth. If you can manage this you can have a go at taking the Golden Fleece – but remember it is guarded by a great serpent which is for ever on the watch. What is more, you must take it yourself; none of your companions may help you.' Jason bravely agreed.

Medea was sitting by her father while all this was going on. She knew full well that what he had told Jason to do was absolutely impossible for any mortal to accomplish. As she saw him standing there, so young and brave, she fell in love with him and decided to use her magic powers to help him. In the evening she went to offer sacrifices to Hecate, the goddess of witches and enchantresses. On the way she met Jason who begged her to come to his aid.

'I will! I will!' she cried, 'I have fallen in love with you and couldn't bear anything to happen to you. But my father will be very angry when he finds out. You must save me from his wrath.' Jason was completely under her spell by this time. 'If you give me your help I will take you back to Greece with me as my bride,' he promised. Medea was overjoyed and gave him the magic herbs he was to use next day.

At sunrise Jason went to the field where the contest was to take place. King Aetes, Medea and all of the people were there to watch. Then came the bulls snorting fire, their horns and hooves made of bronze. His companions watched in terror as Jason went up to the bulls. They expected him to be burnt to death by the fire flaring from the bulls' nostrils and did not know about the magic herbs that Medea had lovingly given him. Much to their amazement Jason was completely unscathed. The herbs had toughened his skin and made him entirely fireproof! Aetes glared angrily as he saw Jason do the impossible and hitch the bulls to the yoke. As he began to plough up the field his friends gave a great cheer of encouragement and hopes began to rise.

Then Jason began to sow the dragons' teeth. For a few moments nothing seemed to be happening, but then the ground began to heave and out of the soil emerged an army of men clad in armour and brandishing weapons. The friends gasped in horror, even Medea looked somewhat shaken, but Jason calmly picked up a boulder and hurled it into the midst of the soldiers. Immediately they began to fight amongst themselves and soon there was not one left alive. King Aetes could hardly believe his eyes.

Now for the serpent that guarded the Golden Fleece. As Jason approached he could see the creature coiled round the trunk of the tree where the Fleece was hanging, his fangs flicking in anticipation. Luckily Jason had with him some of the magic juice from the herbs of forgetfulness Medea had given him. He sprinkled it liberally into the serpent's eyes and as he did so he recited some spells Medea had taught him to say. For the first time ever, the serpent grew drowsy and soon he was fast asleep. Jason crept up to the tree, grabbed the Golden Fleece and ran off in triumph before King Aetes had realised what had happened. 'Quick!' shouted Jason to Medea, 'Let's go!' Together they ran to the ship and soon were sailing far out to sea.

Aetes did not want to give up either the Golden Fleece or his daughter and immediately set out after them in hot pursuit. Medea again came to the rescue. She was so afraid of what he might do that she committed the most terrible crime. On board the *Argo* was her little brother, Absyrtus, whom Aetes loved dearly. She ruthlessly killed him, cut his body into pieces and threw them into the water, knowing her father would stop to gather up the remains of his son so he could bury them decently. Jason and his friends were so terrified of King Aetes that they did not try to stop her, but later, when things went badly wrong for her, people said she was being punished for her dreadful deed.

When they reached Iolcos, Jason and Medea were married. At first they lived happily together and soon they had two little boys. Then, as Medea was madly in love with Jason she committed another terrible crime on his behalf. She thought he would be pleased with her if she took revenge on Pelias for having taken the throne of Iolcos from his father. One day an ideal opportunity arose. The daughters of Pelias came to her saying, 'We have heard you can make old people young again. Could you do this for our father? He is so old we are afraid he might die and we do not want to lose him.' Medea assured them that she could. 'Watch me,' she said, 'I will prove that I can.' With that she took an old sheep, cut its throat and plunged it into a cauldron of boiling water.

Suddenly they heard the sound of bleating and when they looked into the pot they saw, instead of an old sheep, a newborn lamb!

Pelias' daughters were satisfied and led Medea to the room where their old father was sleeping. 'What are you waiting for?' she asked. 'Take a knife and drain out your father's old blood so that I can replace it with new.' Pelias awoke and screamed out in pain, but Medea, ignoring his cries, promptly plunged him into the vat of boiling water that she had brought with her. But this time there was no magical transformation. The old man was dead and Medea had wreaked the revenge she had planned.

The people of Iolcos were revolted at what Medea had done. Although they were very fond of Jason they said he and his wife could no longer live in their city. And so Jason and Medea had to find a new home in Corinth. They had not been there very long when Medea became very unhappy. Jason no longer loved her. He wanted to leave her and marry Glauke, the daughter of the king of Corinth, instead.

Medea could not eat or sleep. She tormented herself continually with the thought that Jason had betrayed her. 'How could he?' she cried in anguish. 'And after all I've done for him! I have left my home and my family. I have committed murder for his sake and this is how he thanks me.' Her friends tried to comfort her, but she was so wrapped up in her agony she did not hear them. They thought she might go out of her mind and feared what she might be plotting.

One day the boys' tutor came to see their nanny. 'How has Medea taken it? Has she stopped weeping yet?' he asked. 'I don't think she will ever stop' the nurse replied. 'Jason has broken her heart.' 'I'm afraid there's worse news to come,' the tutor went on. King Creon says he won't have Medea and the boys in Corinth once Jason is married to his daughter. He is going to throw them out.' 'But surely,' protested the nurse, 'Jason won't stand by and let that happen to his sons even if he has quarrelled with their mother?' 'Unfortunately he will,' the tutor replied. 'All he thinks about is Glauke. He never gives a thought to his children.'

'We must try to keep the boys away from Medea,' said the nurse. 'She has a very cruel streak and is bound to seek her revenge. I sometimes see her looking at them with a very wild look in her eye. And she screams out her hatred of Jason and Glauke too, calling on the gods to grind them to pieces. I dread to think what she might do.'

After a while Medea calmed down and began to be more reasonable. She got up from the bed where she had flung herself in her grief and rage and went outside to speak to the women of Corinth who had gathered outside. 'Life has dealt me a cruel blow,' she said. 'I never expected Jason would treat me like this. He was my whole life as he very well knows. Now I can only look on him with contempt. He has abandoned me for a marriage he thinks will bring him riches. His wife will be a princess and not a refugee, for that is what I am. I have left my native land, my home and my family for his sake. What is to become of me now? What loneliness is there like that of a stranger far from home? I shall have my revenge, never fear, but for the moment, keep silent.'

Just then King Creon arrived and announced that she and the children must leave Corinth at once. 'And when I say at once, that is exactly what I mean. I shall not go back to the palace until I have seen you safely over the border,' he snarled. 'But this is the cruellest blow of all,' said Medea, 'I have absolutely nowhere to go, and besides what have I ever done to make you treat me like this?' 'I don't trust you an inch,' replied Creon. 'I'm afraid you're plotting to harm my daughter. I know you are a witch and can perform all kinds of magic. What is more I have heard your rantings and ravings about getting your revenge so I am not taking any chances. Out you go! And be quick about it!'

Medea then begged him to allow her to stay for just one more day. 'I need to make plans for myself and especially for the children as Jason doesn't seem to have done anything about it. Have pity on them at least. You are a father yourself so you must understand.' Creon reluctantly agreed. 'Very well then you can't do much harm in one day.' Creon was wrong. One day was all Medea needed.

Just as she was congratulating herself on winning this extra time, along came Jason. 'You really are a very foolish woman,' he began. 'If you hadn't made all this fuss you wouldn't have been told to go. Even so I will not see you go short of anything. Indeed the reason for my visit is to bring you this money.' Medea turned on him angrily. 'You filthy coward!' she screamed. 'So you have come at last. It's just as well that you have. Let me remind you of all I have done for you. It will do me good to get it off my chest and I hope it makes you squirm!

You might just remember how I saved your life when you had to yoke those fire-breathing bulls and sow the dragons' teeth, that it was I who gave you the magic herbs to overcome the serpent and take the Golden Fleece. I killed my brother so you could escape my father's wrath and killed again so you could regain your throne. And how have you rewarded me? I'll tell you how! You have abandoned me and our two children into the bargain. Not content with that, for the sake of your latest love you have turned us out into the world alone and friendless.'

'A hard act to follow,' said Jason coldly, 'but don't forget I've also done a lot for you. I brought you here to Greece, to the most civilised land in the world where there is freedom and justice. Now you are famous too. Everyone knows of your magic powers. If you had stayed at home, in the barbarous place you came from, who would have heard of you then? What is more if only you had been reasonable you could have continued to live here in Corinth after my marriage to the princess. Don't you see how much better off you would have been? We hadn't a penny when we came from

Iolcos. When I marry the princess I will be rich and could have afforded all sorts of nice things for you and the boys. They could have been brought up alongside the children Glauke and I will have – the equal of princes. And now, through your jealousy, you have ruined everything. You have no one to blame but yourself.'

After Jason had gone Medea sent for the children's nurse. 'I've got it all worked out,' she said. 'First of all I will send a messenger to Jason asking him to come and see me once more. Then I will butter him up a bit, tell him he was right to act as he did. I will say that I am ready to leave Corinth, but beg him to let the boys stay. Not that I would dream of leaving them here on enemy soil, but I need them to carry out part of my plot. I'll send them to the palace with wedding gifts, a beautiful dress and a gold coronet which will kill Glauke if she puts them on. Then, I must kill my boys, although it will break my heart to do so. No one shall take my children from me. Then I will flee. What do I care for life now? Everything that was precious I lost when I left my father's house to come to Greece with Jason. Now with the help of the gods he will be punished. He will never see our sons alive again, and his new wife will never have a child, but die a terrible death when my poison does its work. Nurse, go and fetch Jason!'

When Jason arrived Medea turned on all her charm. 'Jason,' she said, 'do forgive me. I have always been hot-tempered. Since you were here a short while ago I have been thinking things over. You were quite right; I was stupid to make such a fuss, much better to remain friends.' 'I am very pleased you have changed your mind,' replied Jason. 'Now you are talking sense.'

The boys were playing in the house. Medea called to them to come out. 'Are you there boys?' she called. 'Come and say hello to your father. We have patched up our quarrel. Let's all be friends just like we used to be.' Turning to Jason she went on, 'I realise that after all that has happened I will have to leave Corinth, but the boys would be so much better off here with you. Do ask Creon to let them stay.'

Jason was doubtful but promised to try to get Creon to change his mind. 'Even if you can't, I am sure Glauke could,' wheedled Medea. 'And see here, in these caskets I have some wonderful wedding presents for her, a beautiful dress and a golden coronet. Surely these will do the trick if she needs some persuasion. Come, boys, you can take them to her at once.'

Little did Jason know that the favour he was about to ask would seal his children's fate and cause the death of the princess. After leaving their gifts at the palace the children returned home and went on with their games. Medea, meanwhile, kept gazing out along the road from the palace, longing to hear the news she knew must come. 'Here it is!' she said gleefully as she saw the messenger speeding towards her.

'Escape while you can,' he panted. 'The princess is dead, killed by your poisons.' 'Excellent news! Just what I wanted to hear,' replied Medea. 'Tell me what happened.' So the messenger described how the princess had been won over by the children's smiles. She had accepted the presents graciously and agreed to ask her father to let them stay in Corinth.

Hardly were they out of the palace than she had taken the dress out of the casket and tried it on. Pleased with the effect she next placed the golden coronet on her shining curls and turned this way and that to admire herself in the mirror. Suddenly, a terrifying thing happened. She went white, staggered wildly and collapsed in a chair. Then she began to foam at the mouth. A moment later steam began to hiss out of the coronet and the next the dress burst into flames. Glauke screamed out in pain and her father came rushing in. He tried to save her but as soon as he touched her the flames consumed him too.

Medea knew there was no time to lose. 'The time has come when I must kill the children', she said and went into the house to find them. Jason came tearing along the road. 'Where is she?' he roared. 'She has killed Glauke and Creon with her schemes. She will be punished for this! Where is she I say? Has she escaped? Where are the children? I am much more concerned about them than about her.' He began to hammer on the door with his fists. 'Open the door,' he yelled. 'Open the door! I demand to see my children!'

And then he noticed a chariot drawn by green dragons hovering over the roof. Holding the reins was Medea ready to make her escape. 'What are you doing battering on the door like that? If you want to see your sons they are here in the chariot with me. Do not blame me for their deaths. It was your insult to me that killed them. With that, the chariot rose into the sky and Medea was gone, while Jason stared helplessly after them.

THE ROMAN WORLD

Portrait of a Roman lady.

From Hawara in the Fayum oasis in Egypt (c. AD 160-170).

Chapter 10

Women of Ancient Rome

As is the case with women in Ancient Greece much more is known about women from wealthy families in Rome than women from poor homes. In general Roman upper-class women had more independence than Greek women but even so their main role in life was said to be that of model wives and mothers. This view was often written on gravestones like this one belonging to a lady called Claudia who lived in the second century AD. Her husband said she had loved her husband with all her heart and had given birth to two sons. Apparently she was graceful in her manner and elegant in appearance. She managed the household well and made wool. Spinning and weaving were very high on the list of wifely virtues. Even the emperor Augustus had his wife, Livia, on show in the front hall of their house sitting at her loom where everyone could see her.

However, it seems that not all wives were models of virtue and in the first century BC many were known to have been rather free with their sexual favours. It was often claimed that these women were actresses, escorts and prostitutes but it is known that at least some of them were the wives or widows of Roman senators. Their behaviour was in stark contrast to the laws issued by Augustus in 18 and 17 BC and revised in 9 AD regarding moral and marital conduct aimed at stamping out adultery. This was no longer regarded as a family matter. Severe penalties could be imposed both on the erring wife and her husband. The matter would be dealt with in a public court and husbands and fathers could sentence their wives or daughters and their lovers to death in certain circumstances. At the very least the husband of a guilty wife would have to divorce her or be accused of being a pimp. Both men and women accused of adultery were to be banished to off-shore islands and had their property or dowries taken away.

In contrast to women in the Greek world, Roman women had quite a bit of independence. In Athens in the fifth century BC, for instance, women were expected to stay at home and did not take part in social life where men were present. They did not go to parties, for instance, which were considered to be 'men only' affairs although the men were entertained by call-girls and female entertainers. In Rome women were present at dinner parties and were not relegated to certain parts of the house as they were in Greece. However, there were some restrictions. Augustus passed laws which allowed them to sit only on the back row at the theatre and gladiatorial shows! The women's areas of the public baths were also smaller and less luxurious than the men's.

The relative independence of women is reflected in the Roman rules regarding marriage and women's rights. Women did not take their husband's name when they married and were not completely under his legal authority. If her father died an adult woman could inherit his property. They were allowed to make business transactions in their own right, to buy and sell, to make a will and free slaves. There was one restriction, however. Officially they had to have a guardian (*tutor*) to approve of their dealings, although some wives managed their affairs without. The wife of the senator Cicero, sold a row of houses to raise funds for him when he was in exile and collected the rents from her own estates apparently without a guardian being consulted.

Strangely enough women had much less say when it came to getting married. It was expected that all women would marry without exception, apart from special groups like the Vestal Virgins (see page 85). They also had very little choice about the man they were to marry; in prominent families marriage was often used to put the seal on political or financial deals. For example, the Roman general Sulla tried to get Pompey to support him in his bid for the Consulship by arranging for him to marry his (Sulla's) step-daughter, even though she was married to somebody else at the time and was expecting a baby. Later he married Julia, the daughter of Julius Caesar to seal an agreement of mutual support.

Women seem to have been married on several occasions during a lifetime. A first marriage could take place when the girl was around fourteen or fifteen and parents often started thinking of suitable partners for their girls when they were as young as six, although they would not be actually married for several more years. On the other hand men were usually married for the first time when they were about twenty-five to thirty and would be about ten years older than the bride. A young woman could find herself marrying a much older man if he was getting married for the second or third time.

Some marriages were very happy in spite of the fact they had been arranged by the parents for any but romantic reasons, but divorce was very common. Often this would be because the wife had served her usefulness to one husband and her parents would then have to be looking around for another advantageous union.

As women were expected to produce heirs for their husbands, pregnancy and childbirth must have been constantly on their minds. Most women faced the prospect of years of pregnancies, wanted and unwanted. Apart from abstinence there was little women could do about it. Prolonged breast-feeding may have delayed further pregnancy but this is doubtful. In any case wealthy women would have employed a wet-nurse. There were also highly dangerous methods of abortion available and some weird and wonderful types of contraception.

Not only was childbirth extremely hazardous – it has been estimated that one woman in fifty died giving birth – but childlessness was also a common ground for divorce. Lack of children was always considered to be the woman's fault.

Grief caused by the death of a woman in childbirth was universal. It was certainly not confined to the upper classes as inscriptions written by heartbroken husbands on the gravestones of ordinary women attest. One man writes about his 36-year-old wife who was in labour for three days before she died. It was her tenth delivery. Another says his wife suffered agonies for four days without being able to give birth and then also died.

Women never had political rights or power in Ancient Rome, but several had a great deal of influence. One such was Livia, the wife of Augustus.

Not only did Augustus listen to her advice but he gave her what almost amounted to an official position. She was portrayed in Roman sculpture just like Augustus was and he gave her several legal privileges including sitting in the front row at the theatre and financial independence. She was also given the right of *sacrosanctitas* (protection from attack) which was based on the rights of a male public official, something unheard of for a woman previously. She was even called *Romana Princeps,* the female counterpart of the title of Augustus himself, *Romanus Princeps,* which means First Citizen of Rome. Livia's title meant something like First Lady, the title of the wife of the President of the U.S.A. today.

The reason for this increased status seems to have been that Augustus was keen to found a dynasty which would continue to rule in perpetuity after his death. Livia was the corner-stone of his plan. However, the couple had no children together. According to the Roman historian, Suetonius, Livia had just one premature still-birth while married to Augustus. But Livia had been married before and had a son, Drusus, and was pregnant with another, Tiberius, when she married Augustus who had a daughter, Julia, from a previous marriage. Augustus now had to make use of his relations if he were to found the dynasty he so much desired. So Julia was first married off to her cousin, Marcellus who died when she was only sixteen, and then to Augustus' friend, Marcus Agrippa, who was twenty years older than she was. Finally, she was married to Livia's son, Tiberius, after he was brutally divorced from his wife of whom he was very fond. Augustus let nothing stand in his way as far as the foundation of his dynasty was concerned, but the much desired heirs did not materialise in spite of all his efforts. Julia and Tiberius had one child but he did not survive childhood. In the end Augustus had to adopt Tiberius as his heir while Julia was banished to an island and never allowed to come back to Rome. Apparently she had rebelled against her father's plans for her and is said to have led a wild immoral sex-life in retaliation. She was also accused of treason.

During the Roman Republic (the era before Augustus became emperor) there was a small group of families who controlled affairs in Rome. The women of these households seem to have been in control of social and political matters within their own families. They arranged marriages amongst the younger family members and so made alliances with other powerful families. They also gave moral and financial support to their male relations and their political aims. The famous Cornelia was one of these women. She was very well connected. Her father was Scipio Africanus who had defeated Hannibal in the Punic Wars and she had two sons, Tiberius and Gaius Grachus, who became radical political reformers. Cornelia was praised in ancient times for her devotion to their political education and training. A letter to her son, Gaius, exists which illustrates her ability to communicate and to influence her sons' careers. She was a gracious educated woman who dressed modestly and tradition has it that when her lack of jewellery was commented on she indicated her two sons and said, 'These are my jewels'.

Another very capable and ambitious woman was Fulvia who came from a wealthy and once influential family. She was married first to Clodius, then Curio, two aspiring politicians, and finally Mark Anthony and became involved in the political upheavals of the first century BC. She was not a woman whose only interest in life was running the household and being a model wife and mother, but used her organizational skills to political ends. After she had married Mark Anthony she took part in the civil wars and at one stage (in 40 BC) may have shared command with Lucius Antonius as a military leader in support of her husband against Octavian (later called Augustus). Some historians do not believe that she really did this and that his enemies put the tale about so they could sneer that Lucius had shared his command with a mere woman.

Soon afterwards Fulvia died. Mark Anthony patched up his quarrel with Octavian and sealed the new alliance by marriage to Octavia, Octavian's sister. This may have been a good move politically but Mark Anthony must have been less than serious in regard to Octavia as by this time he had fallen under the spell of Cleopatra who had just had twins by him. However, Octavia proved to be a capable woman as well as a devoted wife in the years ahead.

According to the writer, Plutarch, a few years later Mark Anthony had been angered by the slanderous stories which Octavian had been spreading about him so he gathered together a huge fleet of 300 ships and sailed towards Italy to confront him. When he reached Tarentum, Octavia who was accompanying him persuaded him to let her visit her brother in an effort to reconcile them. She had already had two daughters by Mark Anthony and was again pregnant so when she met him on the way she appealed to him not to make her the saddest woman in the world when she had been the happiest. She pointed out that the eyes of the world were upon her as she was the wife of one of the rulers of the world and the sister of the other. If it should come to war no one would be able to predict who would win, but what was certain was that she would be the most miserable of women. Octavian was touched by her tears and entreaties and he decided to meet Mark Anthony and make peace. Octavia's diplomacy was successful. Mark Anthony invited Octavian to dinner during which Octavian decided to give Mark Anthony two legions for his Parthian campaign and her husband gave Octavian 100 ships. And so they parted on friendly terms, Octavian agreeing to look after his sister and the children.

The Parthian campaign proved to be a disaster, however. Thousands of Roman soldiers were killed in battle or died in the storms and severe weather conditions on the return march. Mark Anthony at one point went down to the Lebanese coast to wait for Cleopatra to bring him reinforcements.

In the meantime Octavia also wanted to go to Mark Anthony. Octavian agreed, not so much to make Octavia happy but to give him an excuse to declare war on Mark Anthony if he didn't treat his sister well. Octavia had collected a large amount of clothing for the troops, many pack animals as well as money and presents for Mark Anthony and his friends, not to mention the 2,000 crack soldiers she brought with her. Octavia was in Greece at this time and was very hurt by letters from Mark Anthony telling her to stay where she was and told her about his plans for his new campaign. She knew what his real reason was – Cleopatra! One of Mark Anthony's friends was sent to tell him about what she had brought and what a wonderful woman she was. Cleopatra was afraid she would lose Mark Anthony if he saw Octavia again and so she inveigled him back to Egypt while her rival remained in Greece.

When Octavia returned from Athens, Octavian was so incensed by Mark Anthony's treatment of her that he advised his sister to leave his house and set up her own home elsewhere. She refused and stayed on in her husband's house and looked after his children, not only those whom he'd had with her but also with Fulvia. She also had her own children from her first marriage and after the death of Mark Anthony and Cleopatra took in their children too. She always entertained any of his friends who visited Rome and interceded for them with Octavian if they were trying to get a post in the government. She was famous for her hospitality and generosity of spirit as well as her loyalty and diplomatic skills.

One group of women who had special status was the Vestal Virgins. They were female priests (all the other priesthoods were composed of men) of the hearth goddess, Vestia. Their main function was to make sure that the fire burning in her temple never went out so that the goddess would eternally protect the city. This priesthood was said to have been founded in ancient times by Numa, one of the earliest kings of Rome and was very important for the Roman state. The Vestal Virgins represented the daughters of the ancient royal house. Originally there were only two of them but in historical times there were six when they served the goddess for thirty years during which they had to be virgins. They were chosen by the chief priest, the *Pontifex Maximus,* There would be about twenty candidates, all between six and ten years old, not necessarily from wealthy families.

The Vestal Virgins had several privileges including exemption from having their fathers as guardians, but they were under the strict control of the *Pontifex Maximus* who could have them whipped if they let the sacred fire go out. If it was discovered they had had sexual relations they could be put to death by being shut up alive in a tomb.

Chapter 11

Cleopatra

There are seven Egyptian queens called Cleopatra. The last one, Cleopatra VII (51-30 BC) is the famous one. Many plays and films have been made about her, books written and pictures painted of her. The period she lived in is called the Ptolemaic period (305-30 BC) because the king who founded it, and all the kings who belonged to it, were called Ptolemy. There were fifteen of them altogether. The other queens were either called Berenice or Arsinoe which makes the history rather difficult to sort out.

Ptolemy was not a king at first. He was one of Alexander the Great's generals. For a time Egypt was part of Alexander's empire. After Alexander died suddenly in 323 BC the empire was carved up by three of his generals and Ptolemy got Egypt. After governing Egypt on behalf of Alexander's descendants for seventeen years he decided to make himself king and reigned as Ptolemy I. He and his son, Ptolemy II, seem to have been capable rulers and achieved a great deal during their time in office. They built Alexandria, the city designed by Alexander but which he never saw materialise. They also constructed the great Library where mathematicians like Euclid and Eratosthenes worked and which housed the plays of the great Greek dramatists like Aristophanes, Sophocles and Euripedes. The famous lighthouse, one of the Wonders of the Ancient World, was built at this time too.

The later Ptolemies were not such competent kings. There was a great deal of in-fighting during this time. Kings and would-be kings had their rivals assassinated and often appealed to the Romans to take their part against their enemies. Rome was expanding at a rapid rate at this time and often intervened as it offered the Roman generals the opportunity to interfere in Egyptian affairs and to make Rome rich from the bribes of the rival kings when asking Rome for aid. This was the situation when Cleopatra first became queen.

Cleopatra at first ruled jointly with her father, Ptolemy XII, and then with her brother Ptolemy XIII. He was only ten years old and Cleopatra herself only eighteen which meant that they were very vulnerable in a society where others wished to take over. As they were so young a Regency Council had been set up to rule on their behalf. Nonetheless, her brother managed to oust her from power for a while. However, the Roman general, Pompey, tried to come to her aid as he had been appointed her guardian after the death of her father. Unfortunately for him, he was defeated by his own rival, Julius Caesar, and fled to Egypt. The Regency Council did not trust him and were afraid he would try to seize power, so they sent one of their officers, ostensibly to welcome him, but who had him murdered as he stepped ashore in Alexandria. Cleopatra fled to Askelon in Palestine and Ptolemy XIII to Pelusium in the Delta.

What happened next is known from the writing of Plutarch who lived in the first century AD that is just over one-hundred years or so after the events he describes.

He wrote a book called *Great Lives* and in it he compared the life and achievements of famous Greeks and Romans. For example he wrote a comparison of Julius Caesar and Alexander the Great, both very famous generals. He also wrote about Mark Anthony, another Roman general who became very powerful after the death of Julius Caesar. Both he and Julius Caesar are also famous for being the lovers of Cleopatra.

However, he did not write a book about Cleopatra herself, so to get to know about her life we have to look for information in the lives of Julius Caesar and Mark Anthony. Plutarch says that four days after the murder of Pompey, Julius Caesar landed in Alexandria where he was offered Pompey's head. According to Plutarch, Caesar refused to look at it but took Pompey's signet ring and sheds tears as he did so. He offered help and friendship to all who had been friends of Pompey and had been arrested by the young king.

Plutarch writes that he then summoned Cleopatra to return to Egypt and that she arrived in a small boat, slipping past the guards rolled up in a sleeping bag carried on the back of her friend Apollodorus. Caesar was captivated by this trick and Plutarch says 'as he got to know her better he was overcome by her charm'. He also arranged for the reconciliation of Cleopatra and her brother and ordered that they ruled jointly as their father had laid down in his will.

However, it wasn't long before Ptolemy XIII rebelled against Caesar and was drowned in a sea battle fighting against him. Caesar could have taken over Egypt at this point, but decided not to. Instead Cleopatra was married to another of her younger brothers, Ptolemy XIV and the agreement again was that they should rule jointly in the spirit of their father's will.

In the meantime, it is obvious that Julius Caesar had fallen in love with Cleopatra and in 47 BC they took a trip up the Nile together. There are no details of the affair in the ancient writers, but shortly afterwards when Caesar left for Syria, Cleopatra had a baby son. She claimed he was Caesar's child and named him Caesarion after his father. Opinion about this was divided at the time. Octavian, who was Caesar's heir, saw the child as a possible rival and would not recognise him as Caesar's, but Mark Anthony did.

In 46 BC Caesar returned to Rome and became dictator. Cleopatra with little Caesarion and her brother, Ptolemy XIV visited him there. Not much is known about this visit except that Caesar paid Cleopatra the compliment of building a small temple in honour of Venus Genetrix who was regarded as the Mother of the Roman people and placed a gilded statue of Cleopatra in it. Many people were offended by this.

During the next two years Caesar seems to have offended many more people by his arrogance and on the Ides of March 44 BC he was assassinated at the foot of Pompey's statue during a meeting of the Senate. Fearing for the safety of her son Cleopatra returned to Alexandria taking Caesarion with her. Ptolemy XIV either died or was murdered and Caesarion became co-ruler of Egypt with Cleopatra.

After the assassination of Julius Caesar war broke out between the Roman generals. Bruutus and Cassius committed suicide and Octavian (Caesar's heir) and Mark Anthony divided the Roman world between them. Octavian took over in the West and he in the East.

Mark Anthony wanted to conquer Parthia. To do this Mark Anthony needed Cleopatra's help and sent her several letters summoning her to Tarsus to meet him. Cleopatra was an extremely clever woman and took her time in coming. When she eventually did it was with an impressive fleet and entourage. Plutarch describes the scene:

She came sailing up the River Cydnus in a barge with a poop of gold, its purple sails billowing in the wind, while her rowers caressed the water with oars of silver which dipped in time to the music of the flute, accompanied by pipes and lutes. Cleopatra herself reclined beneath a canopy of cloth of gold, dressed in the character of Venus as we see her in paintings, while on either side, to complete the picture stood small boys dressed as cupids, who cooled her with their fans. Instead of a crew the barge was lined with the most beautiful of her ladies-in-waiting attired as Nereids and Graces, some at the rudders, others at the tackle of the sails, and all the while an indescribably rich perfume, exhaled from innumerable censers was wafted from the ship to the shore.

The whole scene was so beautifully stage-managed that huge crowds were attracted, some people sailing alongside her from the mouth of the river, and when news reached the town of her arrival, others left the market place and came down to meet her. In the end poor Mark Anthony found himself sitting there all by himself waiting for Cleopatra to appear. Cleopatra had won hands down!

She gained the upper hand again later when he invited her to dinner. She declined the invitation and replied that it would be more appropriate if he came to her. Her aim was to show off and point out that he was only a rough soldier and that she did these things in a much more civilised manner. Again Plutarch says:

He found the preparations made to receive him magnificent beyond words, but what astonished him most of all was the extraordinary number of lights. So many of these, it is said, were let down from the roof and displayed on all sides at once, and they were arranged and grouped in such ingenious patterns in relation to each other, some in squares and some in circles, that they created as brilliant a spectacle as can ever have been devised to delight the eye.

Next day he invited her to a banquet where he hoped to surpass the splendour and elegance of her arrangements. Plutarch says that,

he was hopelessly outdone in both and was the first to make fun of the crude and meagre quality of his entertainment.

Cleopatra quickly learned how to handle him.

Cleopatra saw that Anthony's humour was broad and gross and belonged to the soldier rather than the courtier, and she immediately adopted the same manner towards him and treated him without the least reserve.

In paintings Cleopatra is always depicted as being a very beautiful woman, but Plutarch says she wasn't especially beautiful in the usually accepted sense. This is certainly borne out in the few authentic ancient images that exist today. On coins, which are the best likeness of her, she has a beaky nose and a determined chin. However, Plutarch says she had other charms.

...there was an attraction in her person and her talk, together with a peculiar (special to her) force of character which pervaded her every word and action, and laid all who associated with her under its spell. It was a delight merely to hear the sound of her voice with which, like an instrument of many strings, she could pass easily from one language to another.

Plutarch was particularly impressed with her ability to speak several languages. She could speak Ethiopian, Hebrew, Arabic, Syriac, Persian and Parthian to mention only a few and she spoke them so well she rarely needed an interpreter. She had also taken the trouble to learn the Egyptian language something her predecessors had never bothered to do. He says they couldn't even speak their own language properly.

At any rate Mark Anthony was completely captivated even though he was married to a Roman lady called Fulvia at the time and who was conducting two military campaigns on his behalf, one in Italy to protect her husband's interests there, and another on the border with Syria. In spite of this Mark Anthony allowed himself to be 'taken prisoner' by Cleopatra and carried off by her to Alexandria where he wasted his time in frivolous amusements. Apparently he and Cleopatra gathered a group of friends round themselves, the Inimitable Livers, and gave incredibly extravagant banquets in honour of one another every day.

Cleopatra was not wasting her time, though, rather she was biding her time. Eventually Mark Anthony was to give her Syria as a gift instead of presenting it to Rome. Meanwhile, Anthony's wife, Fulvia, had been stirring up trouble in Rome by going to war against Octavian, thinking that this was the best way to make her husband leave Cleopatra. She sent him a letter saying she had been defeated and begged him to come back to rescue her. This he set out to do and he and Cleopatra did not see each other for the next three years. During this time, Fulvia died. Mark Anthony patched up his quarrel with Octavian and married his sister, Octavia.

Cleopatra does not appear to have been jealous of Fulvia. Plutarch reckons she always said she had every reason to be grateful to her:

Fulvia was a woman who took no interest in spinning or managing a household, nor could she be content to rule a husband who had no ambition for public life. Her desire was to govern those who governed or to command a commander-in-chief. And indeed Cleopatra was indebted to her for teaching Mark Anthony to obey a wife's authority, for by the time he met her, he had already been quite broken in and schooled to accept the sway of women.

Not only that but Cleopatra knew exactly how to maintain her hold over Mark Anthony. Again, Plutarch explains:

Plato says there are four kinds of flattery, but Cleopatra knew a thousand! Whether Mark Anthony's mood was serious or merry she could always find some fresh device to amuse or charm him. She engrossed his attention utterly and never released him for a moment either by day or night. She played dice with him, drank with him, and hunted with him, and when he exercised with weapons she would watch him.

He used to like to go out at night dressed up as a slave when he would wander the streets peering in through people's windows and shouting rude comments. Cleopatra would go with him disguised as a maid servant and join in the ribaldry. She also liked a joke at Mark Anthon's expense. One day he went out fishing and was very annoyed because he caught nothing and Cleopatra was watching. So he told some fishermen to dive down into the water and fasten some fish they had already onto his hooks so that he could 'catch them'. When he brought them up Cleopatra pretended to be taken in although she guessed what had happened, so she invited her friends to come fishing with them again the next day. This time she got her servant to fix a kipper onto Anthony's line. When he pulled it up everyone burst out laughing and Cleopatra told him to leave fishing to the fishermen and to stick to 'catching' cities and continents.

Mark Anthony spent three years in Rome with his new wife Octavia and when he went back to Syria he went alone, but as the coast of Syria came into sight his fatal fascination for Cleopatra overcame him and he sent for her to come to join him. He is said by some to have married her and he certainly showered lavish presents upon her. In addition to the lands she already possessed he gave her Phoenicia, Central Syria, Cyprus, Judea, as well as parts of Asia Minor and the Arabian coast. By waiting patiently and stringing Mark Anthony along she had got what she wanted – to increase Egypt's possessions in the East. By giving these lands to Cleopatra Mark Anthony offended his countrymen back home. To make matters even worse in their eyes he acknowledged as his the twins he had had with Cleopatra. The boy he named Alexander Helios (the Sun) and the girl, Cleopatra Selene (the Moon).

The Parthian Campaign was a disaster involving heavy losses in spite of the fact that he had mustered such a vast army that Plutarch says it *'alarmed even the Indians and made all Asia tremble'*. And this was all because of his adoration of Cleopatra:

Such was his passion to spend the winter with her that he took the field too early in the season and conducted the whole campaign in a disorderly fashion. It was as if he were no longer the master of his own judgement, but rather under the influence of some drug or magic spell, for he gave the impression that his eyes were constantly drawn to her image and his thoughts fixed upon hastening his return rather than upon conquering the enemy.

In Rome, Octavian made much of Mark Anthony's failures and reviled him for his desertion of his wife. Octavia was well aware of her husband's infidelity and was determined to sail east to try to get him back. Octavian allowed her to do so thinking that if Mark Anthony treated her badly it would give him an excuse to declare war on him. When Octavia arrived in Athens she received letters from her husband telling her to stay where she was and explained his plans for a new expedition. Octavia saw through Mark Anthony's excuses but even though she was very hurt she wrote back asking where she should send all the supplies she had been collecting – clothing for the troops, many pack animals, money and presents for his friends and best of all, 2,000 crack soldiers all equipped with full armour.

Cleopatra could see the way things were going and was afraid that she might lose Mark Anthony to her rival if he were to spend any time with her. So Cleopatra made a great fuss, declared she was desperately in love with Mark Anthony, and ate hardly anything so that she began to waste away. When he appeared she gazed on him in rapture and when he left looked to be on the point of collapse. Whenever she saw him she seemed to be crying but would brush away her tears as if she didn't want him to see. She kept up this performance all the time he was preparing for his new campaign and at the same time her supporters kept telling Mark Anthony what a brute he was to neglect her so shamefully. They said that his marriage to Octavia was only a marriage of convenience for the sake of her brother. She had been given the honour of being called a wife whereas Cleopatra who was the ruler of many nations had been content to be his mistress. She was absolutely devoted to him and here he was killing her!

In the end he believed them and went back to Alexandria with Cleopatra while Octavia returned alone to Athens whereupon her brother claimed that she had been grossly insulted and prepared for war against Mark Anthony. This war culminated in the sea battle of Actium which ended in total defeat for Mark Anthony and Cleopatra. Plutarch says that Cleopatra insisted on a sea battle, not because that would give them the best chance of winning but that it would provide her with an escape route if things went wrong.

Neither side seemed to be winning for a while, then suddenly to everyone's amazement, Cleopatra's sixty ships hoisted sail and made off straight through the middle of the battle causing chaos. Mark Anthony then showed how completely under Cleopatra's spell he was by abandoning and betraying the men who were fighting and dying for him and, escaping in a five-banked galley with only two supporters, blindly set off after *the woman who had already ruined him and who would soon complete his destruction.*

Cleopatra signalled to him to come aboard her ship which he did but made no contact with her. Instead he sat by himself in the bows holding his head in his hands bemoaning his fate while the ship sailed towards Libya.

Meanwhile Anthony's fleet managed to fight on for several hours against Octavian until a gale blowing against them forced them to surrender. Very few people knew that Anthony had fled and when the news got out no one could believe it as a large part of his army was still undefeated.

When Anthony landed on the coast of Libya he sent Cleopatra back to Egypt while he wandered about accompanied by just a couple of friends. The news began to come in that his supporters had defected to Octavian. Mark Anthony tried to commit suicide. His friends stopped him, however, and persuaded him to go back to Alexandria. Here he was welcomed by Cleopatra and even though he knew the rulers of all the territory he had once conquered had rebelled against him he seemed not to care and embarked with her on another bout of extravagant banquets. They were thought to have made a pact to die together and to enjoy what was left of their lives.

Meanwhile Cleopatra was collecting all sorts of deadly poisons and tested them out on prisoners who had been condemned to death to see which was the least painful. She found that the bite of the asp was the best as it brought on a kind of drowsiness and numbness and was not in the least painful.

They also sent messengers to Octavian asking that Cleopatra's children should inherit the throne of Egypt and that Mark Anthony should be allowed to retire from public life and go to live in Athens as a private citizen. Octavian refused Mark Anthony's request but told Cleopatra she could have anything she liked provided she would put Anthony to death or make him leave Egypt.

Mark Anthony believed that to fall in battle was the most honourable way to die and so he went to war again against Octavian. At first he was successful but later his navy, infantry and cavalry all deserted him and went over to his rival, Anthony was beside himself with rage and blamed Cleopatra for his humiliation. Cleopatra was terrified and fled to the tomb she had been building and locked herself in. She then sent messengers to Mark Anthony to tell him she was dead.

When Mark Anthony got the message he decided to kill himself as he no longer had any reason to continue living. Sometime in the past he had made a pact with his faithful servant, Eros, who agreed to kill him if the need arose. He then sent for Eros and told him the time had now come. Eros took out his sword but instead of instead of killing his master he turned the sword away from him and stabbed himself. Mark Anthony then tried to kill himself but only managed to wound himself badly. He began to cry out in agony and when Cleopatra heard about this she sent orders to bring him to the tomb. The doors remained locked but when Cleopatra looked out of the window she let down ropes and ordered slaves to raise him up. She herself also hauled on the ropes to pull him up. Plutarch described the scene:

Those who were present say there was never a more pitiable sight than the spectacle of Anthony, covered in blood, struggling in his death agonies and stretching out his hands towards Cleopatra as he swung helplessly in the air. The task was almost beyond her and it was only with great difficulty that she managed it. When she had got him up and laid him on a bed, she tore her dress and spread it over him, beat and lacerated her breasts, and smeared her face with the blood from his wounds.

Anthony had scarcely breathed his last when Octavian heard about all this on his arrival in Alexandria and sent one of his officers to the tomb to bring back Cleopatra alive so she could be shown off in his victory parade. She refused to surrender but the officer got inside by a trick. He persuaded her that Octavian meant her no harm and told her she was to be treated with the respect due to a great queen. She was also allowed to give Anthony a splendid funeral and had him buried in her own tomb.

While she was still mourning Mark Anthony, Octavian came to see her. She seemed to be much changed having given up her extravagant life-style and was lying on a straw mattress dressed only in a simple tunic. As Plutarch says, *her hair was unkempt and her expression wild, while her eyes were sunken and her voice trembled uncontrollably.* However she was soon up to her old tricks; when Octavian entered she threw herself at his feet. He urged her to lie down and came to sit close beside her, whereupon she began trying to justify her part in the war saying she had been forced into it by Mark Anthony. Octavian clearly didn't believe her so she quickly changed her tune and threw herself on his mercy with prayers and pleading. In the end she gave him a list supposedly of all her treasures. One of her servants gave her away and said it wasn't quite complete. Cleopatra went for him grabbing him by the hair and pummelling him in the face. Octavian was amused by this, especially when she said,

Isn't it outrageous that when you do me the honour of coming to visit me in my wretched condition that I should be accused by my own servants of keeping a few trinkets back? They weren't for me, I assure you, but for Octavia and your wife, Livia, so that I could appeal to them to make you kinder and more merciful.

Octavian was pleased that she seemed to be making plans for the future and he told her she could trust him to deal with her more generously than she might have thought possible. So off he went thinking that he had pulled the wool over her eyes whereas it was really the other way round.

Soon after he had gone Cleopatra began making arrangements for her death. First she had a bath, then lay down and was served with an exquisite meal. Just then an Egyptian peasant arrived with a basket of figs. The guards were suspicious that they contained some kind of poison, but the man let him sample them and finding nothing amiss they let him in to the queen. She then sent a message to Octavian asking that she should be buried next to Mark Anthony. After this she sent all of her attendants away except for her two faithful ladies-in-waiting, Iras and Charmian. Then she closed the door of the tomb. When Octavian read the message he sent messengers to the tomb to see what was going on. They were too late. When they burst in they found Cleopatra lying dead upon a golden couch and dressed in her royal robe, her maids dying at her feet.

Tradition has it that she killed herself by letting an asp bite her breast. The guards had been right to be suspicious, but wrong about the figs. There was indeed nothing wrong with the figs but what they didn't realise was that there was an asp hidden among them.

So, do we admire or condemn her? Was she an unscrupulous, immoral woman?

Or did she use her feminine charms in the interests of Egypt?

Chapter 12

Boudicca – leader of resistance to Rome

Boudicca was leader of the British tribe, the Iceni, who occupied territory in south-east Britain. The Romans under the emperor Claudius had conquered Britain in AD 43. He seems to have been very anxious to be seen as a military hero and came to Britain in person for a short time – accompanied by elephants which must have been a source of amazement to the people to say the least.

Back in Rome he was personally unpopular and may have hoped that this victory would show him in a better light. However, that may be, he called his son Britannicus to emphasise the importance he laid on this event.

The conquest was carried out with great harshness and eventually the people rebelled. The Roman historian Tacitus recorded the many uprisings in his book *The Annals of Imperial Rome* which deals with Roman history from the end of the reign of Augustus to that of Nero. Tacitus knew a great deal about Britain as he was married to the daughter of Agricola, the Roman Governor, and his account of the rebellion seems to be reliable.

The Iceni, although they had earlier voluntarily agreed to become allies, rather than enemies, of Rome, nonetheless decided to rebel. However, at this stage they were easily defeated and their defeat made some of the other tribes less anxious to declare war for a time. Not so another British tribe, the Silures, and the fear of them led the Romans to found a settlement of ex-soldiers at Camulodunum (Colchester) to keep control on their behalf. Meanwhile the military commander, Ostorius, invaded the territory of the Silures whose leader was Caratacus, one of the most famous leaders of

British resistance to Rome. He was not only a very brave man but was good at military strategy and knew the area where he wanted to fight very well. Tacitus says he was very cunning and always chose as a battlefield a site that had many advantages to himself and none to the Romans. In spite of this and the huge amount of support from neighbouring tribes he was defeated and taken as a captive in chains to Rome. Together with his wife, his daughter and his brothers he was paraded through the streets in the victory procession. By this time the fame of Caratacus had spread far beyond Britain and had even reached Italy. In Rome everyone came out to see the man who had been stirring up trouble for the Romans for the last nine years..

Surprisingly, he did not look at all down-cast at his treatment and when he reached the platform where the emperor was sitting on his throne he spoke these words:

Coming as I do as a king, if I had been only moderately successful, I should have come to this city as a friend rather than an enemy and you would have been glad to have me as an ally…As it is, humiliation is my lot but glory yours. I had horses, men, arms and wealth. Are you surprised I am sorry to lose them? If you want to conquer the world does it follow that everyone else welcomes enslavement? If I had surrendered without striking a blow before being brought before you, neither my downfall nor your victory would have become famous. If you execute me both will be forgotten. Spare me and I shall be an everlasting token of your mercy.

Claudius was so impressed he pardoned him and his family.

However, back in Britain the resistance went on, mostly in the form of guerrilla warfare in woods and marshes. The Silures were exceptionally stubborn and determined to make the Roman commander eat his words. He had been declaring frequently that the Silures must be completely exterminated, but instead the Silurians had begun to muster more support from other British tribes. Ostorius died, worn out with his impossible task and another commander, Didius, was appointed. He was not pleased to find on his arrival that the Roman army had suffered more defeats and when it came to subduing the Britons he was no more successful than his predecessor had been.

Later he was replaced by Suetonius. He was anxious to cover himself with glory and decided to attack the thickly populated island of Mona. The Romans built flat-bottomed boats which could be used to carry the foot-soldiers over the shallow water to the island. Then came the cavalry. Sometimes their riders swam alongside the horses. The Romans were confronted by a great crowd, among them women dressed in black and with dishevelled hair so they looked like witches. They were brandishing flaming torches. Next to them were the Druids, *raising their hands to heaven and screaming dreadful curses.* This scene scared the Romans at first but Suetonius urged them on telling them not to be afraid of a bunch of hysterical women. As they were better armed the Romans won in the end and Sutonius destroyed the sacred groves of the Druids and left a garrison behind to maintain control after he had left.

While Suetonius was dealing with the island of Mona he learnt of trouble elsewhere in the province. Sometime earlier, the king of the Iceni tribe, Prasutagus, had made a deal with the Romans. Prasutagus was a very successful and prosperous tribal king. He decided it would be better policy to make friends with the Romans than to regard them as an enemy, so he made the arrangement with them that after his death his daughters and the Roman emperor would rule the tribe jointly. He thought this was the best way to make sure his people and his daughters would be safe from attack. How wrong was it possible to be? After his death in AD 60 his kingdom and household were brutally attacked. His widow, Queen Boudicca, was beaten within an inch of her life and her two daughters were raped. The other chiefs of the Iceni had their lands confiscated and the king's other relatives were made slaves.

These humiliations led to a great revolt and the rebels marched on Camulodunum, regarded as a symbol of domination by a foreign power. The focus of their hatred of this settlement of ex-soldiers was the temple of the Emperor Claudius who was considered by the Romans to be divine. People said that the cost of the cult was draining Britain of her resources. Here Boudicca and her allies were able to destroy the town fairly easily as the town had no defensive walls. They were encouraged in their attack by the fact that suddenly, for no apparent reason, the statue of the god of Victory fell down and other strange signs and portents occurred. The sea turned red and the corpses left behind by the receding tide were left on the river banks. These were all thought to be signs that the Britons would win and the Romans defeated and, fortunately for them, it certainly turned out to be the case.

Even though Camulodunum was destroyed by the rebels Suetonius marched relentlessly on to Londinium, an important centre for business and trade which Boudicca also attacked. As he did not have enough soldiers to capture the town he left thinking it as better to sacrifice this one town in order to save the province as a whole. He advanced to Verulamium (St. Alban's) where again Boudicca and the other supporting tribes wreaked havoc.

In order to rally support Boudicca and her daughters rode in a chariot all round the neighbouring countryside encouraging the other tribes to join the revolt:

'We British are used to woman army commanders' she cried. *'I am descended from mighty men. But now I am not fighting for my kingdom and wealth. I am fighting as an ordinary person for my lost freedom, my bruised body, and my outraged daughters. Nowadays Roman rapacity does not even spare our bodies. Old people are killed and virgins raped. But the gods will give us the vengeance we deserve! The Roman division which dared to fight is annihilated. The others cower in their camps, or watch for a chance to escape. They will never face even the din and roar of our thousands, much less the shock of our onslaught. Consider how many of you are fighting – and why! Then you will win the battle or perish. That is what I as a woman intend to do – let men live in slavery if they will.'*

However, Suetonius told his men to ignore Boudicca's battle cry and urged them to fight as they had never done before. This they did and soon all serious resistance was overcome. Even the women and baggage animals were not spared and added to the heaps of the dead. Tacitus says they won a glorious victory, the Britons losing 80,000 men compared to the Roman 400.

In despair Boudicca killed herself by drinking poison. As a Roman, Tacitus was recording events as he saw them, and was probably somewhat prejudiced in favour of Rome. Nevertheless he was broad-minded enough to express his admiration for a brave enemy.

Chapter 13

Zenobia – rebel queen of Palmyra

Zenobia was famous as a courageous queen who challenged the power of the Romans in the third century AD when Rome was experiencing all sorts of difficulties. There was civil war, the generals were fighting each other for control of the empire and the economy was very unstable. She certainly took advantage of the situation to establish herself as the ruler of the eastern part of the empire.

It is very difficult to find any reliable information about her as the historians who wrote about her lived a long time after her death. She is mentioned in the *Historia Augusta* (a collection of biographies of the emperors from AD 117-284) which was written in fourth century. The historian Zosimus is late 5th century while Zonares wrote in the 12th century. An Arab writer, Al-Tabari, wrote between six and seven-hundred years after the events he describes. Not surprisingly some of the stories they record are rather fanciful.

Palmyra is in Syria and was a very important place in the third century. It was close to a great oasis and was a huge merchant city on the route from Homs to Dura Europos on the Euphrates. From there the route led south to the Gulf, the Indian Ocean and all the markets of the east in one direction. Westwards, as the Silk Road, it went to the great trading centres of the Levant and eventually to Rome. It was well placed to provide the empire with the luxury items its citizens demanded – spices, perfumed oils, ebony and ivory, precious stones, glass and even silk from China. After the Romans conquered the Nabataeans in the second century, they diverted trade from Petra (the Nabataean capital) to Palmyra which then became more important than ever.

Zenobia was born in Palmyra, which was in the Roman province of Syria, round about 240 AD. She was named Julia Aurelia Zenobia after some famous Romans from whom her father claimed descent. Later Zenobia claimed the legendary Dido of Carthage and Cleopatra among her ancestors. Her parents were Roman citizens and so Zenobia was entitled to be one too.

According to the Arab writer, Al-Tabira, Zenobia was put in charge of her family's flocks and their shepherds at a young age and that is why she became so good at controlling men, and excellent at horse riding too. During this time she developed the stamina and endurance she was later famous for. He claimed she could march for miles with her soldiers, could hunt as well as any man and out-drink anyone.

In his *Rise and Fall of the Roman Empire* the 18th century writer, Edward Gibbon, has a high regard for her (although he doesn't seem to think much of women in general calling them servile and indolent). He says she was just as beautiful as her ancestor, Cleopatra but far surpassed her in chastity and valour.

He goes on: *Zenobia was deemed the most lovely as well as the most heroic of her sex. She was of a dark complexion. Her teeth were of a pearly whiteness and her large black eyes sparkled with uncommon fire, tempered by the most attractive sweetness. Her voice was strong and harmonious. Her manly understanding was strengthened and adorned by study.'*

She seems to have been good at Latin and Greek as well as the Syrian and Egyptian languages, was very knowledgeable about history and could discuss the relative merits of Homer and Plato. Gibbon seems to have got his information from the much earlier *Historia Augusta* and this perhaps explains the regard in which Zenobia was held in both ancient and modern times.

By AD 258 Zenobia had married Lucius Septimus Odaenthus, the Roman governor of the province of Syria. They had a son named Vaballathus. Zenobia was his second wife and Odaenthus had another son, Herodes, from his first marriage. At this time Odaenthus ruled over the important trading city of Palmyra and all the area round about. Merchants coming along the Silk Road to Rome or returning from there had to pay taxes on the goods they brought with them so Palmyra became very wealthy. However, some of the Persian kings, the Sassanids, were jealous of the prosperity of Palmyra and the surrounding area and blocked the trade routes from time to time so that the people of Palmyra could not obtain the taxes. This annoyed the Roman emperors and in AD 260 the emperor Valerian marched against the Sassanids, but he was defeated by them and taken prisoner. Odaenthus came to the rescue. He successfully marched against the Sassanids and drove them back across the Euphrates. The Romans were so grateful for this they made him governor of the whole of the eastern part of the Roman Empire. Odaenthus became even more powerful when there was trouble between the next emperor, Gallienus, and Quietus who wanted to rule instead. Again Odaenthus turned up trumps and went to the emperor's aid. As a result Odaenthus was given the title of *Corrector of the East* and was able to rule almost independently of Rome.

However, a few years later, Odaenthus quarrelled with his nephew and was assassinated by him. Herodes, his son by his first wife, was killed at the same time. In the past it was often said that Zenobia had a hand in this as she wanted her husband's powerful position for her own son, although this is not the view of most modern historians.

Either way Zenobia then acquired a taste of power herself. Her son, Vaballathus, took over nominally as ruler in his father's stead but, as he was still a child, Zenobia became regent and ruled on his behalf. She continued her husband's friendship with Rome hoping to gain further advantage from this policy. During the past few years 26 men had come and gone as emperor and she may have felt her son was in with a chance of being the next if she played her cards right. In fact she seems to have been so ambitious she may have even fancied her own chances.

In the five years after her husband's death she worked hard at gaining a reputation as mistress of the East. She lived a sumptuous lifestyle and established a brilliant court of philosophers and writers, and also became known as a formidable army commander. As her confidence grew she began to challenge Rome itself and in AD 269 sent her army into Roman Egypt and claimed it as her own. Even this could have been explained away as Zenobia's acting in the interests of Rome rather than her own. A revolt against Roman rule had broken out while the Roman Governor had been away on campaign so she could maintain that she had gone to the aid of Rome. On the other hand, some people think she might have stirred up the revolt herself in order to have an excuse to invade Egypt.

After her success in Egypt, Zenobia then turned her attention to the Levant and Asia Minor (modern Turkey) and added them to her rapidly expanding empire.

The Romans at this point were too occupied with their own political and economic problems to do anything about Zenobia's increasing power. By the time of the Roman Emperor, Aurelian, Zenobia had had coins minted with Aurelian's head on one side and that of her son, Vaballathus, on the other as joint rulers of Egypt. She also she gave her son the title of Augustus and assumed the title of Augusta herself. These were titles that only the Roman Emperor and his family were allowed to use. Zenobia had clearly overstepped the mark here and relations with Rome began to deteriorate.

Emperor Aurelian was much more successful than his predecessors and by AD 272 had defeated many of his northern enemies and was ready to deal with Zenobia. He invaded Asia Minor and destroyed all the towns and cities loyal to her until he reached Tyana where the philosopher Apollonius lived. He is said to have appeared to Aurelian in a dream and advised him to be merciful to the city. Aurelian admired Apollonius and so took his advice. When the other cities saw that Tyana had been spared they decided to follow suite and surrendered to Aurelian and transferred their allegiance to him.

He then marched on Palmyra. It is not known whether Zenobia tried to negotiate with him before he reached the city. The *Historia Augusta* records a letter Aurelian sent her at the beginning of his campaign demanding her surrender and her arrogant reply, but this is now thought to be a bit of artistic licence put into the account to contrast the emperor's reasonable approach with Zenobia's arrogance.

When Zenobia had news of Aurelian's advance she rallied her troops and marched to meet him. Aurelian won by pretending to retreat and then swung round to face Zenobia's army when the men were exhausted from chasing after them. Many of her soldiers were killed but Zenobia herself fled to the city of Emesa where she had more troops and where her treasury was. Aurelian pursued her to Emesa and again defeated her army by using the same tactics as before. Yet again Zenobia escaped and managed to reach Palmyra where she organised the city's defences. Aurelian followed behind and laid siege to the city. Zenobia seems to have been hoping for reinforcements to come from Persia. When they did not materialise she fled with her son on the back of a camel to seek sanctuary in Persia. After Palmyra fell and Aurelian realised she had gone he sent his cavalry after her. She was caught and taken prisoner while trying to cross the Euphrates to safety. She was brought back to Aurelian in chains and finally taken to Rome.

Accounts differ about what happened when she got there. Zosimus says she and her son drowned in the Bosphorus while on the way to Rome. The *Historia Augusta* states that she was paraded through the streets of Rome in gold chains and dripping with jewellery during Aurelian's victory parade after which she was released, given a pension and ended her days in 'peace and luxury' in a villa at Tibur near to Rome. Zonaras claims she was indeed taken to Rome but never took part in Aurelian's victory parade. Later she married a wealthy Roman while Aurelian married one of her daughters.

The Arabic version is even more colourful. This claims she married a tribal chief, Jadhima, but murdered him on their wedding night. His nephew determined to have revenge followed her to Palmyra whence she fled on a camel to the Euphrates. Earlier she had taken the precaution of building a tunnel under the river but unfortunately was captured just as she was about to enter it. She then killed herself by drinking poison or in yet another version of the story she was executed. So you can take your pick; it all depends on which story you find the most credible!

Whatever we make of the stories surrounding her end Zenobia was clearly a formidable woman and was much admired in later times. One of the most famous people who did so was Lady Hestor Stanhope who visited Palmyra in 1831. She was a legend in her own lifetime, a bizarre, extraordinary women, very self-willed and self-confident. She seems to have fancied herself as a second Zenobia. A niece of William Pitt, she had had a very privileged upbringing and later acted as hostess for him. After his death she spent the money he had left her, and that of the father of Michael Bruce, her escort and lover, on extensive tours in the Middle East. Breaking all sorts of social and religious conventions on her visits to Constantinople, Cairo and Damascus, she eventually arrived in Palmyra and described her entrance into the city as the greatest triumph of her life. *'I carried everything before me,* she wrote, *and was crowned under the triumphal arch.'* Dr Meryon, a member of her retinue, was perhaps a little nearer the truth when he wrote that the local inhabitants did their best to welcome her by putting on an entertainment which involved an imaginary attack on a caravan. He was somewhat worried that the drama might turn into the real thing! However, she was led down into the ruins where she expressed an interest in all she saw. As they went down Colonnade Street young girls draped and garlanded had been perched on the brackets of the columns to add to the effect of her reception. When she reached the Triumphal Arch, apparently, they all jumped down and danced and sang. Then they turned into the Temple of Bel where the whole village turned out to greet her. Or so she said!

THE 19th AND 20th CENTURIES

Chapter 14

Amelia Edwards

Amelia Edwards was a Victorian lady who became very interested in the Ancient World, particularly Egypt, and did a great deal to help preserve the monuments that she saw being destroyed by Western dealers and collectors as the European countries vied with each other to create the most impressive museums. She wrote several books about her travels elsewhere, but her most famous one was called *A Thousand Miles up the Nile*. This is a fascinating account of her adventures on her trip up the Nile beginning in December 1873 and continuing until the following summer. Very few women at that time would have attempted anything like this. All of the quotations in this account of her life are taken from her book.

However, she first became interested in Egypt completely by chance. She and a friend had gone to France on a sketching holiday and, much to their disgust, had been plagued by weeks of rain. After discussing *whether to take our wet umbrellas back to England* or to *push on further still in search of sunshine* they decided to go to Egypt. She later wrote:

For in simple truth we had drifted hither by accident, with no excuse of health or business or any serious object whatsoever, and had just taken refuge in Egypt as one might turn aside into the Burlington Arcade – simply to get out of the rain.

In spite of this, once there, it was clearly a case of love at first sight. On looking out of her window the first morning she was immediately captivated by the scene:

It was dark last night and I had no idea that my room overlooked an enchanted garden, far-reaching and solitary, peopled with stately giants beneath whose tufted crowns hung rich clusters of maroon and amber dates. It was a still warm morning. Grave grey and black crows flew heavily from tree to tree and perched upon the topmost branches. Yonder between the pillared stems rose the minaret of a very distant mosque; and here where the garden was bounded by a high wall and a windowless house, I saw a veiled lady walking on the terraced roof in the midst of a cloud of pigeons. Nothing could be more simple than the scene and its accessories; nothing at the same time, more Eastern, strange and unreal.

Her enthusiasm grew with her first visit to the Cairo bazaar:

Every shop front, every street corner, every turbaned group is a ready-made picture. The old Turk who sets up his cake stall in the sculptured doorway, the donkey boy and his gaily caparisoned ass, waiting for his customers; the beggar asleep on the steps of the mosque; the veiled mother filling her water jar at the public fountain – they all look as if they had been put there expressly to be painted.

It is easy to see why her book was a best-seller when it was published in 1876. Amelia had the happy knack of being able to put her finger on the very thing the traveller has observed, perhaps unconsciously, but would have found difficult to put into words. For instance she expresses disappointment at the distant view of the Pyramids of Giza;

The well-known triangular forms are too familiar to be in anyway startling. There is no way of scaling them against any other object so it is impossible to appreciate their true size. But then, as we get nearer, we begin to see they are not so familiar after all. When at last the desert edge is reached and the long sand-slope climbed and the rocky platform gained, and the Great Pyramid in all its unexpected bulk and majesty towers above one's head, the effect is as sudden as it is overwhelming. It shuts out the sky and the horizon. It shuts out all the other pyramids. It shuts out everything but the sense of awe and wonder.

She goes on to say that all the careful studying of maps and plans does nothing to prepare us for the actual sight of the pyramids. We all think we know there are three pyramids but when we get there we find there are nine. Surrounding them is a rocky plateau covered with the remains of numerous tombs of the men who served the kings who had the Pyramids built. She complains that this *is not the desert of our dreams.*

Moreover we are not really prepared for the rugged appearance of the Great Pyramid. It had been stripped of the outer blocks in the Middle Ages to build mosques and palaces when Cairo was first built so that now it looks like a giant staircase. But she says it doesn't look like a ruin either. *It looks as if it had been left unfinished and as if the workmen might be coming back tomorrow morning.*

It is typical of her enterprise and courage that she decided to make the most of her trip by hiring a *dahabeeya* (a flat bottomed boat) and engaging a captain and crew with a view to sailing to Aswan and even further into Nubia.

This was fraught with difficulties. She says buying a house is bad enough but buying a *dahabeeya* is a hundred times worse. For one thing *boats keep changing their positions which houses do not do* and how *to compare boats with six cabins and boats with eight; boats provided with canteen* (a galley) *and boats without; boats that can pass the cataract* (a barrier of rocks stretching across the Nile) *and boats that can't; boats that are only twice as dear as they ought to be and boats with that defect five or six times multiplied.*

Eventually she and her friend found one to their liking and the day for departure arrived. After scurrying off to the shops to make a few last-minute purchases they went on board and immediately set about transforming *the comfortless hired look* of the dahabeeya's saloon into a cosy Victorian parlour.

As Amelia remarks, *it is wonderful what a few books and roses, an open piano and a sketch or two will do.*

Amelia was a keen observer of the weaknesses of human nature and was able to laugh at her own. In the early part of her book she describes how their departure from Cairo was being celebrated with a splendid lunch when suddenly they were disturbed by the sound of shots. These proved to have been fired by a French party who were pointing out they were getting one over on the English by sneakily leaving first while they were busy eating. Laughing at herself she writes:

I fear that we being mere mortals and Englishwomen could not help feeling just a little spiteful when we found the French had started first; but then it was a consolation to know that the Frenchmen were only going to Assuan. Such is the esprit du Nil. The people in Dahabeeyas despise the Cook's tourists; those who are bound for the Second Cataract look down with lofty compassion upon those whose ambition extends only to the First; and travellers who engage their boat by the month hold their heads a little higher than those who contract for the trip. We who were going as far as we liked for as long as we liked could afford to be generous. So we forgave the French and went down again into the saloon and had coffee and music.

It may seem as though Amelia Edwards was merely a leisured Victorian woman with plenty of money and time on her hands to engage in frivolous activities. Far from it. One of her most endearing qualities was the respect she showed for the people she met and those who served her needs on the *dahabeeya*. On her first visit to the Sultan Hasan Mosque, in her opinion the most beautiful in the Moslem world, she was not only impressed by the purity of the architecture but by the *unaffected reverence of the Moslem at prayer*.

This was the first time we had seen Moslems at prayer and we could not but be impressed by their profound and unaffected devotion. Some lay prostrate, their foreheads touching the ground; others were kneeling; others bowing in the prescribed attitudes of prayer…We did not know then that the pious Moslem is as devout out of the mosque as in it; or that it his habit to pray when the appointed hour comes round, no matter where he may be or how occupied. We became so familiar, however, with this trait of Mohammedan life that it seemed quite a matter of course that the camel driver should dismount and lay his forehead in the dust by the roadside; or the merchant spread his prayer carpet on the narrow mastaba (bench) of his little shop in the public bazaar; or the boatman prostrate himself with his face to the east, as the sun went down behind the Libyan hills.

Her sympathy with the Egyptians who made her journey possible is equally clear. She was obviously moved by the stories of her crew:
One man was born a slave and will carry the dealer's brand marks to the grave.

Another has two children in Miss Whateley's school in Cairo. A third is just married and has left his young wife sick at home. She may be dead by the time he gets back and he will have no news of her meanwhile.

Others told her of their horrific struggles to pay the taxman and their fear of being called up for forced labour for the government. *The poor fellows were ready enough to pour out their hopes, their wrongs, their sorrows. Through sympathy with these one comes to know the men and through the men the nation.* These feelings are in sharp contrast to the colonial views held by many at this time.

By far the greater part of her book is devoted to the monuments. She describes traipsing across the desert *in all the blaze of noon* to visit the impressive tomb of the Fifth Dynasty high official Ti. He was a priest and a commoner but important enough to the king to have had the honour of marrying his daughter.

Of the façade of the tomb which must originally have looked like a little temple only two pillars remain. Next comes a square courtyard surrounded by a roofless colonnade, from one corner of which a covered passage leads to two chambers. In the centre of the courtyard yawns an open pit, some twenty feet in depth, with a shattered sarcophagus (coffin) *just visible in the gloom of the vault below. In the passage and in the large chamber we find a succession of carved reliefs so numerous it would take half a day to see them all…Here as in a book we have his biography. Ti was a wealthy landowner. He owned flocks and herds and servants in plenty. Here are the oxen ploughing; the owner is scattering seed; the reaper cuts the corn; cows are crossing a stream…the carpenters are fashioning new furniture; the shipwrights are busy with boats. He was fond of fishing and fowling and sometimes used to go after crocodile and hippopotamus.*

In other words we see everything Ti thought he would need in his Afterlife being provided.

Amelia made a thorough study of many of the sites spending day after day among the ruins…*sketching now here, now there, going over the ground bit by bit comparing every detail.*

What is even more interesting is that when her party reached Abu

Simbel she went in for a bit of excavation of her own. One of her friends she nicknamed *The Painter* had gone for a stroll simply to admire the view. On the way back he noticed a rock face sticking up above a mound of sand and on the rock face were some hieroglyphs and the damaged outlines of what had once been carvings of people. He returned to the boat to fetch help and set off again with two of the crew. The others sat down to lunch without him, but immediately abandoned their meal on receiving a note from him requesting sandwiches and saying he had discovered a tomb. Amelia describes what happened next:

In less than ten minutes we were there, asking breathless questions, peeping in through the fast widening aperture and helping to clear away the sand. All that Sunday afternoon, heedless of possible sunstroke, unconscious of fatigue, we toiled upon our hands and knees...under the burning sun. We had all the crew up, working like tigers. Everyone helped, even the dragoman (guide) *and the two maids. More than once when we paused for a moment's breathing space, we said to each other, "If only those at home could see us now, what would they say!"*

And now, more than ever, we felt the need of implements. With a spade or two and a wheelbarrow we could have done wonders; but with only one small fire shovel, a birch broom, a couple of charcoal baskets and about twenty pairs of hands, we were poor indeed. What was lacking in means was made up for in method. Some scraped away the sand; some gathered it into baskets; some carried the baskets to the edge of the cliff and emptied them into the river... Meanwhile the opening grew rapidly bigger

It seems clear now that what they had found was a little painted chapel with a painted frieze running round just under the ceiling and decorated with carved reliefs on the walls *gorgeous with colour*. When the whole party had taken a look the opening was blocked up for the night to prevent anyone getting in and damaging the decoration.

One of the most amusing episodes in her book is her description of her party's spring-cleaning of one of the four enormous statues of Ramesses II that adorn the façade of the main temple at Abu Simbel where they were moored for three weeks. The sailors began to get bored and *The*

Painter decided to set them on to clean the northernmost one which had been disfigured by the plaster left on it when Mr Hay (an early archaeologist) had taken a cast fifty years before.

A scaffolding of spars and oars was at once improvised, and the men, delighted as children at play, were soon swarming all over the huge head, just as the carvers may have done in the days when Ramesses was king.

All they had to do was to remove any small lumps of plaster that might still adhere to the surface and then tint the white patches with coffee…It took them three afternoons to complete the job and we were all sorry when it came to an end.

Except for the cook that is – he was aghast at the vast amounts of coffee that Ramesses consumed. He had never before had to cater for a guest whose mouth measured three and a half feet in length!

On her return to England she began to work on her book *A Thousand Miles up the Nile*. In order to do this she read widely, consulted respected Egyptologists about historical detail and archaeology and learnt hieroglyphs. She soon became an authority in her own right.

Her greatest work was the founding of the Egypt Exploration Fund (now Society). During her travels in Egypt she had been very much concerned about the state of the ancient monuments. Many were suffering from neglect; others were being vandalised. The Egyptian Government had neither the interest nor the resources to protect them.

About the little chapel she and her party had discovered at Abu Simbel she wrote:

I am told that the wall-paintings we had the happiness of admiring in all their freshness are already much injured. Such is the fate of all the monuments great or small. The tourist writes all over them with names and dates…The student of Egyptology by taking wet paper 'squeezes' sponges away every vestige of the original colour. The collector buys and carries off everything of value that he can get…Everyday more inscriptions are mutilated, more tombs robbed and sculptures defaced. The Louvre contains a full length portrait of Seti I cut bodily from his tomb in the Valley of the Kings. The museums of Berlin, Turin and Florence (she might have added the British Museum) *are rich in spoils which tell their lamentable tale. When science leads the way is it wonderful* (surprising) *that ignorance should follow?*

And so in 1879 Amelia wrote to Mariette, the founder of the Cairo Museum, to ask whether he thought it might be possible to finance excavation in Egypt in the Delta by public subscription in England. His reply no longer exists but was presumably favourable as Amelia then wrote to a number of English Egyptologists to canvass their support.

Her most enthusiastic supporter was Sir Erasmus Wilson, an eminent surgeon with a great interest in Egypt. He was writing a popular history of Egypt and had just spent £10,000 transporting Cleopatra's Needle to England. They became great friends after her book *A Thousand Miles up the Nile* was published. He was so impressed by it he wrote to the publisher to ask for her address. She would help him with his book and he always supported her work in Egypt.

Others were less easy to persuade. In the British Museum the Oriental Department (Egypt and the Near East combined) was totally opposed to Amelia's efforts. She was not a recognised scholar and a woman into the bargain so what did she know about Egypt? However, help came from elsewhere in the Museum, from R. S. Poole in the Department of Coins and Medals. To cut a very long story short the E.E.F was set up in March 1882. Poole and Miss Edwards were the Honorary Secretaries and Erasmus Wilson was the Treasurer.

By now Mariette had died and had been replaced by Maspero. He was all for allowing the British to dig in the Delta but absolutely against them taking any finds out of Egypt. This posed a financial problem because the British Public would want to see how their money had been spent before they donated any more. Eventually a deal was struck and the British could take anything the Cairo Museum did not want so the public were satisfied.

Nonetheless, finance continued to be a worry. Erasmus Wilson died in 1884 without altering his will in favour of the fund, something which he had always said he would do. So instead of finding themselves financially secure the Fund now found their main source of income abruptly cut off. However, several members of the committee came to the aid of the Fund. The Reverend H.G. Tomkin gave lectures on Biblical Archaeology, a favourite topic at that time. Miss Margaret Harkness and Miss Helen Burke gave Lectures for Ladies at the British Museum. Admission was by ticket and they gave half of the proceeds to the Fund. Amelia herself worked tirelessly for the Fund making several tours of the northern industrial towns where much of its support came from.

Meanwhile the Fund had been gaining ground in America and in 1889 Amelia embarked on a highly successful but exhausting lecture tour of The States. During the five months she was there she lectured 115 times and travelled to sixteen different states. Everywhere she went her lectures were widely acclaimed and the subscriptions flowed in.

At home, however, things did not always go so smoothly. Relations with the British Museum continued to be strained and scholars elsewhere poured scorn on the Fund *'whose members seem to be elected for distinction in any other science BUT Egyptology'*. Amelia was also hurt by the fact that as she lived out of London matters were often decided behind her back.

In October 1891 she caught a lung infection from which she never recovered. She had gone to Millwall docks to supervise the arrival of antiquities from Egypt and their distribution to various museums. Her strenuous tour of America had already seriously damaged her health and she should never have gone to Millwall, but felt she must out of duty to the Fund. She died the following spring, leaving in her will money to found the first Chair of Egyptology in the country, at University College, London. She insisted that Flinders Petrie, her protégé and by then a famous archaeologist, should be the first professor. You can see many of his finds in the Petrie Museum at University College. Her books became the nucleus of the Egyptology Department Library, now in the Institute of Archaeology at U.C.L.

I, for one, have a great deal to thank her for.

Gertude Bell (1868 -1926)

in her desert kit

Chapter 15

Gertrude Bell

Gertrude Bell was an intrepid traveller, archaeologist and writer who lived in the later 19th and early part of the 20th century. Her achievements were especially remarkable as at that time most women lived very restricted and sheltered lives mostly concerning themselves with home and family. However, Gertrude Bell was no ordinary woman and seems to have been of the opinion that what applied to other women didn't apply to her!

Her early life was conventional enough. She was born in 1868 in Washington Hall in the north of England. Her grandfather, Sir Isaac Lowthian Bell was a wealthy businessman who made his money in the iron and steel industry. He was also an MP and from him she seems to have inherited an interest in the world around and international politics. Her father, Sir Hugh Bell, was a well-off mill owner, but one who cared about the well-being of his workers. Her mother, Mary Shield Bell died giving birth to a son, Maurice, when Gertrude was only three. That she lost her mother at such an early age may account for the fact that throughout her life she was very close to her father.

When Gertrude was seven her father married again and her step-mother, Florence, also had a lot of influence on her ideas especially regarding women's education. Florence wrote children's books and plays. She also wrote a report on Hugh Bell's factory workers and was involved in local affairs with the wives of the workers at the Bolkow-Vaughn iron foundry nearby.

Not surprisingly she did not go to school but like many girls in her situation was educated at home. When she was fifteen she went to London, to Queen's College, to prepare for going to university. She turned out to be a very good student and was the first woman to gain a first-class degree in Modern History at Oxford. Although it is hard to believe this nowadays she was not allowed to receive her degree because she was a woman! However, that made her more determined than ever to do anything and everything she wanted to and so embarked on a remarkable career.

After she left Oxford she travelled to Tehran in what was then Persia (now Iran) to visit her uncle Sir Frank Lascelles who was the British Minister (Ambassador) there. Very few women travelled in the Middle East at that time and such a venture would have been thought most unsuitable for a woman. Gertrude was fascinated by everything she saw and seems to have fallen love with the Middle East from the moment she arrived. She described her adventures in her book, *Persian Pictures* which was published in 1894. From then on she travelled widely in the desert regions of Greater Syria, visited archaeological sites, studied the culture of the various countries she visited and very importantly, she learnt Arabic. One reason why she was able to survive in what was very much a man's world was that she could communicate with the men she came into contact with.

In many ways she was a romantic figure and seems to have regarded herself as 'Queen of the Desert'. She travelled with a great entourage of servants, male guides, and camels and their drivers. She also took the precaution of taking valuable gifts with her to ease her way into the company of the local leaders that she met. Throughout the Middle East she was known as 'El Khatun' which means 'Lady of the Court'. In her diary she wrote of her visit to Baghdad in 1921 and claims that she was received like royalty:

As we rode through the gardens of the Karradah suburb where all the people know me and salute me as I pass, Nuri said, 'One of the reasons you stand out so is because you are a woman. There are lots of political officers but there's only one Khatun. So for a hundred years they will talk of the Khatun riding by.'

And Gertrude agreed with him!

As well as being very well informed about the people and places she visited in the Middle East she was also a brave and highly skilled mountaineer. Between 1899 and 1904 she conquered a number of mountains in Europe including Mont Blanc and others in the Bernese Oberland. She was the first person ever to have climbed some of them. One of these was named after her, the Gertrudspitze. In 1902 she nearly lost her life when trying to climb the Finsteraahorn. Bad weather forced her to abandon the attempt and she had to spend forty-eight hours hanging onto a rope attached to her guides and clinging to a rock face in terrifying conditions – in snow, hail and lightning.

However, she is most famous for her travels in what was then known as Greater Syria which included Syria as it is known today, but also modern Lebanon, Palestine, Israel, Jordan and Turkey. She recorded all the details of her travels in her best known book, *The Desert and the Sown,* and when this was published in 1907 her lively and accurate descriptions opened up a whole new world to people in the West. From this time she also began to visit archaeological sites such as Carchemish on the River Euphrates and Babylon and even worked with archaeologists such as T.E. Lawrence, perhaps better known as Lawrence of Arabia and David Hogarth.

When the First World War broke out in 1914 Gertrude Bell asked for a posting to the Middle East, but this was considered to be too dangerous for a woman and she went instead to France to work as a nurse with the Red Cross.

However, because she was able to speak several languages, including French, German, Italian, Persian, Arabic and Turkish and was very knowledgeable about the Middle East, the different tribes she came into contact with, the geography of the area, and about local politics, she was later asked to work for the British Intelligence Service who realised she could be very valuable to them. Her first job was to lead soldiers through the desert areas. Then in 1915 she was sent to Cairo to work at the Arab Bureau with Lawrence and Hogarth where she helped to protect British interests in the Middle East. Because she and Lawrence knew the Middle East so intimately it was hoped they would encourage the local tribal leaders to join forces with the British against the Ottomans (Turkish rulers) who at this time controlled much of the area. This they did on the understanding that after the war an independent Arab state would be set up.

Because Gertrude knew the area better than any other Westerner, the following year she was suddenly sent to Basra in modern Iraq. The British had captured this port in November 1914. Her remit was to advise the Chief Political Officer, Percy Cox, on local affairs and conditions. She worked for him two days a week making maps to enable the British soldiers to reach Baghdad in safety. While employed by the Arab Bureau she also became Sir John Philby's field controller and introduced him to the finer points of dealing with the local tribes. During the First World War she was the only woman ever employed as a political officer by the British forces and was given the title Liaison Officer.

She was also the only British officer who was remembered by the Arabs with anything like affection.

After the British army captured Baghdad in 1917 Gertrude was summoned there by Percy Cox and given the title 'Oriental Secretary' because of her knowledge of the Arab world. Later, in 1921, she, Lawrence and Cox were invited by Winston Churchill to a conference in Cairo to try to sort out the political situation in the Middle East now that the war had ended. In the event the promised Arab State was never set up and many people in the Arab world felt they had been betrayed. Instead some areas were to be given to the British and French to supervise as mandated territories while new countries like Iraq and Transjordan came into being. Gertrude was sometimes called 'the Kingmaker' as she was instrumental in seeing that Abdullah (Transjordan) and Faisal (Iraq) became kings of the new countries. They were the sons of the leader of the revolt against the Turks, Hussein bin Ali, ruler of Mecca.

Until her death in 1926 Gertrude continued to work in Baghdad in an advisory capacity. She gave King Feisal advice about local conditions, for example, on which parts of the country were traditionally inhabited by certain tribes and about local business arrangements and even told him which people he should appoint to his cabinet and other positions of authority. However, she did not find King Faisal easy to get on with and vowed she was going to give up king making. She later wrote:

126

You may rely on one thing – I'll never engage in creating kings again; it's too great a strain.

She also continued to take an interest in cultural affairs and was responsible for the setting up of the Baghdad Peace Library. This was a private library at first but later was taken over by the Iraqi government and became known as the Baghdad Public Library and from 1961 as the National Library of Iraq.

Gertrude had always been interested in archaeology and had often taken part in 'digs' herself, like the ones already mentioned. She was particularly concerned about preserving the archaeological heritage of Iraq and worked to set up what is known today as the Iraqi Museum. This contains treasures such as those from the Royal Graves of Ur (about 4,500) and impressive wall-carvings from the Assyrian palaces of great kings like Sennacherib and Ashurbanipal. (You can see objects from the same places in the British Museum too.) One of the wings of the Iraqi Museum is named after her.

Her personal life was not so successful. She had two unhappy love affairs but never married or had children and after 1915 when the man she loved was killed in the Gallipoli Campaign she consoled herself by throwing all her energies and great qualities into her work.

She returned briefly to Britain in 1922 when she had to face ill-heath and family problems. The family fortune had dwindled away because of the economic conditions after the end of the First World War. Returning soldiers had expected they would come home to a better life and their disappointment on their return often led to strikes. The financial situation gradually worsened and eventually led to the Great Depression of the 1930s.

When Gertrude returned to Baghdad she soon developed pleurisy. Not long afterwards she was saddened by the news that her half-brother Hugh had died of typhoid. She was found dead in Baghdad on 12th July 1926. Apparently, she had taken an overdose of sleeping pills but whether accidently or deliberately is still a matter of debate.

She was buried in the British cemetery in Baghdad and her funeral was treated as a very special occasion. Her colleagues and other officials attended the ceremony while King Feisal watched her funeral procession pass by from his private balcony.

Her colleague, David Hogarth wrote a tribute to her saying:

No other woman in recent times has combined her qualities — her taste for arduous and dangerous adventures with her scientific interest and knowledge, her competence in archaeology and art, her distinguished literary gift, her sympathy for all sorts and conditions of men, her political insight and appreciation of human values, her masculine vigour, hard common sense and practical efficiency — with feminine charm and a most romantic spirit.

A hard act to follow! Her colleagues echoed Hogarth's feelings at the time and she is still spoken of with admiration in Iraq today where she is regarded as an astute political analyst and competent administrator. It is considered to be a great compliment when a woman is compared to her.

WOMEN ARCHAEOLOGISTS TODAY

Hourig Sourouzian
*is the director of the excavations at the Colossi of Memnon on the
West Bank of the Nile in Egypt.*

Chapter 16

Hourig Sourouzian

Women are doing invaluable work in archaeology today. In this final chapter we look at the work of several women who are working in vastly different areas of Egypt at sites which were flourishing at different periods of Ancient Egyptian history. One of them is Hourig Sourouzian who is the director of excavations at the site of the funerary temple of the New Kingdom king, Amenhotep III (1390 – 1352) on the West Bank of the Nile opposite the modern town of Luxor. It was where daily offerings of food and drink were offered to the dead king to sustain him in the Afterlife and is situated near to the Western Valley, an offshoot of the Valley of the Kings where the king was buried. It was the largest temple ever built in Egypt, 500 metres long (E-W) and 700 metres wide (N-S), but until recently only the two colossi (enormous statues of the king) which once adorned the main gateway were visible. These statues were 20 metres tall and each weighed 1,000 tons. They provide a clue as to the grandeur of the original temple which the king himself describes in an important inscription now in the Cairo Museum. He tells of the wonder of the temple which was built of sandstone overlaid with gold, the many statues which 'reached up to heaven', the flagstaffs which adorned the entrance gate and the ornamental pool just outside.

Dr Sourouzian has been working since 1989 to restore the temple to its former glory. First of all the ground had to be surveyed to test the viability of excavating the site. The actual excavations began in 1998 when the area had to be cleared of reeds, camel thorn and mud. A grid was then made to cover the site and any visible remains like column bases and large pairs of feet belonging to statues marked on it. In 2002 a truly remarkable discovery was made when the remains of another colossal statue came to light. It had once stood outside a second great entrance gate but now had to be rescued from the mud and salty water in which it lay. Because she had the famous colossi to compare it with Dr Sourouzian suspected the statue of the king would have the figure of a queen at his side and bravely went further down to see if she was right. She was rewarded with the discovery of the diminutive Queen Tiye by the king's left leg. It was then covered with sand to protect it until conservation work could begin. The following season pieces of the southern companion colossus were discovered, with again, a very well-preserved statue of Queen Tiye standing on the right of the king. These two colossi have gradually been assembled and raised in their original position at the second pylon of the temple.

Four years later she began a de-watering project in the open courtyard and columned hall of the temple. It was necessary because the water table in the area is very high and this not only makes excavation difficult but the water seriously damages the stonework. Trenches were dug to take perforated water pipes and manholes. This meant taking up some of the pavement slabs and foundation blocks so the excavators could investigate below. The slabs were numbered so they could be re-laid later in the correct order. One of the trenches was found to contain many pieces of quartzite statues and a head of Amenhotep III in three pieces. They have now been re-assembled and the head is considered to be the best likeness of this king ever found. Another pit was packed with statues of the lioness-headed goddess, Sakhmet. Altogether 248 of these statues have now been found from the pit and elsewhere on the site. Sakhmet was a very fierce goddess. She was thought to be a bringer of disease but also regarded as a goddess of healing. There seems to have been plague in Egypt during the reign of Amenhotep III so perhaps he thought he should get into her good books by paying her lots of attention!

In 2007 a number of torsos of red quartzite were found and strangely enough the British Museum has the head which belongs to one of them. The Museum agreed to make a cast of it and this is now joined to the body and the whole re-erected in the open courtyard along with others. More recently a huge alabaster colossus was found with the distinctive features of Amenhotep III. It is the largest statue ever found made in alabaster and is eighteen-metres tall. The head alone is three-metres high and almost as wide.

An extremely important part of the work is the conservation and detailed recording of the pieces found. Many of the statues found had been shattered by an earthquake in 1200 BC and have had to be painstakingly put back together again. As recently as 2017 the lower part of an alabaster colossus of Amenhotep III was lifted out of the water into which it had collapsed. This enormous and tremendously heavy block was raised into an upright position by means of airbags and manpower. A crane was then used to lift it out of the water onto dry land when the cleaning and conservation processes could begin.

It was also carefully and thoroughly documented by means of photography and 3D scans.

And so the work goes on at what was earlier listed by the World Monuments Watch as 'one of the world's one-hundred most endangered sites' and is impressively being restored to its former splendour.

Chapter 17

Penny Wilson

Penny Wilson is Field Director of the excavations at Sais in the Delta sponsored by the Egypt Exploration Society (founded by Amelia Edwards in 1882). In the 26th Dynasty (664 – 525 BC) Sais was a very important city. It was where the kings of this dynasty came from and it became the capital of Egypt during the time they were in power. Herodotus, the Greek historian of the Fifth Century BC, mentions some of its features in his work, *The Histories*. He talks about a royal palace and the royal tombs which were inside the precinct of the temple of Athena whom the Egyptians knew as Neith. (The Greeks often linked their own gods and goddesses with Egyptian ones. The Egyptian goddess, Neith, was a goddess of war and weaving, as was the Greek goddess, Athena.) He also mentions great obelisks and statues, one of which was made of gold which King Amasis made out of an old footbath! There was a great lake too on which the Mysteries of Osiris took place. Unfortunately, although he says he knows what went on there he isn't going to tell us what it was because it was too holy a subject to reveal!

None of these features is visible today although 19th century travellers such as John Gardner Wilkinson and Jean-Francois Champollion (who did most to decipher hieroglyphs) reported seeing huge enclosure walls and mudbrick buildings when they visited the site.

The area today known as Sais lies to the north of the modern village of Sa el-Hagar. It is interesting that the ancient name of the city was Sa and a reminiscence of that survives in the modern name. The modern village stands on a low mound overlooking the Great Pit, a huge depression filled with pools of water, marshy areas, great granite blocks and a basalt sarcophagus (outer coffin).

When Penny Wilson started her work there in 1997 her first job was to survey the site using geophysical and drill core techniques rather than begin excavation straight away because much of the original site lies under agricultural land where rice and cotton are grown. Some of the work had to be carried out in a short space of time because they had only two days between the harvesting of one crop and the sowing of the next. The most spectacular results came from a field near the tomb of a local sheikh where computer analysis of the magnetometer data showed that there were buildings in the ground below. The core drills also found pottery and stone work three to four-metres below the surface.

In her search for the once great capital city Penny Wilson began her excavation work in the Northern Enclosure. Here her team managed to find the last traces of once massive mud brick walls which surrounded a vast enclosure around 700 metres by 680 metres in size. Unfortunately, there were few other indications of royal occupation as the palace and temple of the 26th Dynasty had long since been removed. The only finds were shattered stone fragments from monuments and pieces of pottery.

Underneath the 26th Dynasty city, however, were earlier towns built one on top of the other and excavations have discovered a storage complex from the time of Ramesses II (1279 – 1213 BC) with a Third Intermediate Period (1069 – 664 BC) on top of it – the proto capital of Sais.

The team next began to explore the 'Great Pit' which lay to the south, an area about four-hundred-metres square. Here the team found evidence that huge stone buildings had once stood in this area, Large stone blocks, part of a massive entrance gate were also found and led them to suspect that they had found one of the temples Herodotus mentions.

Archaeology is much more than looking for spectacular finds and Dr Wilson's next task was to locate the city where the people had lived and this involved investigating an industrial site and the town rubbish dump. A great deal of Greek and Palestinian pottery was found and proved that Sais had once been a great trading centre.

But what about the occupation of the city before and after the Saite period? By excavating the foundations of another building on the eastern side of the Great Pit it was found that Sais continued to be occupied in a later period, the Ptolemaic period. There is also evidence for the existence of the town in Roman times. The modern village of Sa el-Hagar actually stands on a mound containing the remains of several settlements from the Saite period to the present day. Strangely enough, evidence for the former splendour of Sais often comes in the form of architectural carved stone blocks which have been removed from their original buildings and are now to be found re-used in the present day houses in Sa el-Hagar itself and the surrounding villages.

The early history of Sais is even more amazing. Further work in the Great Pit shows that there was a settlement here in the New Stone Age (4200-3900 BC) which is the oldest settlement known on the Nile flood plain. The site was also occupied in the Pre-Dynastic period, the Old and Middle Kingdoms and the Second Intermediate period. In fact, putting all the evidence together it can be seen that there has been a settlement of some sort on this site from the Neolithic period throughout the centuries to the present day.

One knotty problem remains to be solved – how to reconcile the needs of the present day villagers and the urgency to protect the archaeological site. Penny Wilson is concerned about both. As she says, Sa el-Hagar is a rapidly growing thriving town and there is a great need for land for building houses, a hospital and a school for the children. She hopes that by carrying out a detailed survey it will be possible to identify the areas of archaeological importance and working together with the local authorities and villagers to draw up a co-ordinated building and site management policy – together.

Chapter 17

Anna Stevens and the Amarna Team

Another very important archaeological site is at Amarna in Middle Egypt. It was briefly the new religious capital of Egypt during the reign of Akhenaten who was probably the father of Tutankhamun. Amarna stretches for about eight miles along the Nile and several teams of archaeologists are working on various parts of the site. Virtually all the archaeologists are women.

Because the Ancient Egyptians knew that life depended on the sun they worshipped the sun in many different forms. The main ones were Khepri, the beetle-headed god who represented the early morning sun, Re who symbolised the midday sun and was represented by a disc, and Atum who is always shown as an old man leaning on a stick and represents the sun in the evening. In the Underworld the sun god is called Re-Horakhti and is depicted as a falcon with the disc of the sun on his head. He sheds his light on the dead as he passes through the Underworld and brings them back to life again. The king is always closely associated with the sun-god. One of his titles is Son of Re and sometimes he is regarded as the sun-god himself.

Akhenaten preferred to get away from the various forms of the sun-god and to concentrate on the more abstract idea of the creative power of the sun which he symbolised as a sun disk. It was called the Aten. This had rays coming down from it and these ended in little hands some of which held an *ankh,* which is the hieroglyph for 'life'. The hands hold the *ankh* to the noses of the royal family to give them life as they raise their hands in adoration of the god. Here the Aten wears a uraeus, the cobra which spits at Egypt's enemies. Usually this is part of the king's headdress. The name of the Aten is also written in cartouches in these scenes, again a practice which is usually reserved for kings. So it begins to look as if the Aten was king of Egypt too and Akhenaten was also the Aten.

In order to practice his ideas Akhenaten left the old religious capital of Thebes and moved to Amarna. This was way out in the desert where no one had ever lived before and where other gods had never been worshipped. He dedicated the new city to the Aten.

The city was occupied for only about twenty years and abandoned shortly after Akhenaten died when much of it was deliberately destroyed. For the last forty years Barry Kemp and his team have been working to reveal the remains. As well as two temples to the Aten there were palaces, the homes of officials, a village where the workers who built the city lived and four cemeteries where the ordinary people were buried.

Anna Stevens is Assistant Director of the Amarna project and has recently been working on the North Tombs Cemetery. In her excavation report Anna says that after seven weeks of digging fifty-five new graves were revealed. These tombs were unusual in that they all proved to be of children and young adults from seven to twenty-five-years-old rather than of people with a wide range of ages. Between 4,000 and 5,000 bodies were buried there, mostly simply wrapped in a piece of reed matting and supplied with few or no grave goods. This is quite unlike most burials from other parts of Egypt where great care has been taken to preserve the body by mummification and to lay it to rest in a beautifully decorated tomb stocked with supplies of food and drink to sustain it in the Afterlife.

Fortunately, the team were able to investigate nine graves that had not been robbed either in the remote past or more recently which was not the case in other places on the site. These graves belonged to sixteen young people and had been dug into coarse gravel-rich sand. It seems this was hard to dig because most of the graves were very shallow and some appear to have been too small as the bodies had had to be squashed in. Five of these graves contained more than one body some of which were wrapped in a single piece of matting, which indicates that they were buried at the same time.

However, there was one exception to the general practice here. Much more care had been taken in one case to prepare the body for burial. Here it had been carefully laid out and was wearing a necklace of glass and faience beads as well as a scarab amulet. This would have been an important part of the funerary equipment as it was thought to prevent the individual being found guilty when he had his heart weighed to see if he had committed any wrong-doing during his life on earth which would stop him enjoying a blissful Afterlife. The body was also wrapped in two layers of matting which shows that more care was taken over this burial.

Generally speaking, though, it is very unusual to find so many young people buried in one cemetery and buried so simply. Why would this have been? It has been suggested that this was because of an epidemic, but if that was so you would expect people of all ages to have been affected by it, especially babies and old people. The conclusion that Anna and her team have come to is that they died so young as a result of the severe conditions under which they worked which would leave them less able to resist infection.

Gretchen Dabbs is Director of Bioarchaeology at Amarna and she agrees. She has examined the skeletons of children (some as young as seven) and young adults unearthed here and has found that these show serious injuries to limbs and arthritis of the joints caused by extremely hard and difficult work. She also found evidence of poor diet which would have made them less resistant to disease and thinks that the multiple burials can be explained as those of people dying about the same time and buried in the same grave for the sake of convenience. Gretchen also suggests that the apparent lack of care over the burials could be explained by the fact that the occupants were living at some distance from their families.

The team have also been concerned about the publication of their work at the South Tombs Cemetery. How were they to help readers imagine what it looked like in antiquity when it lay in a more or less featureless desert location with few grave markers and almost no grave goods? They decided to enlist the help of Fran Weatherhead who had done splendid work on their behalf previously when she had produced a very important study of wall-paintings from the city and, later, a beautiful water-colour reconstruction of the Main Chapel at the Workmen's Village. By carefully studying the finds from the cemetery Fran has been able to produce a painting which illustrates the remoteness of the cemetery and the simple nature of the burials with their few grave markers and the possible ceremony when the body was laid to rest and offerings brought to provide for them in eternity.

The work of these women makes it clear that archaeology is not all about the treasures of Tutankhamun. Their many skills and sheer hard work is importantly revealing what it must have been like to be a working person at Amarna in the 14th century BC.

If we should find it hard to visualise children as young as seven working on a building site we must remember the children who worked in the factories and coalmines of Victorian England.

Bibliography

THE MIDDLE EAST
Women in Mesopotamia
Amelie Kuhrt	*The Ancient Near East*	Routledge	1995
Leo Oppenheim	*Letters from Mesopotamia*	Chicago	1967
Karen Radner	*Ancient Assyria*	O.U.P	2015

The Palace of Mari
Stephanie Dalley	*Mari and Karana*	Longmans	1984
Amelie Kuhrt	*The Ancient Near East*	Routledge	1995
Leo Oppenheim	*Letters from Mesopotamia*	Chicago	1967

Semiramis, Queen of Assyria
Amelie Kuhrt	*The Ancient Near East*	Routledge	1995
P. Bienkowski &			
A. Millard (Ed)	*Dictionary of the Ancient Near East*	B.M.P	2000
I.L. Finkel &			
M.J. Seymour (Ed)	*Babylon, Myth and Reality*	B.M.P	2008

EGYPT
Women of Deir el-Medina
A.G. McDowell	*Village Life in Ancient Egypt – laundry lists and love songs*	O.U.P	1999

Hatshepsut the Female Pharaoh
A.M. Dodson	*Monarchs of the Nile*	Rubicon Press	1995
W.C. Hayes in	*Cambridge Ancient History Vol. II Part I*	C.U.P	1973
J. Tyldesley	*Hatshepsut*	Penguin	1999

The God's Wife of Amun
G. Robins in	*Images of Women in Antiquity* (Ed. A.Cameron & A. Kuhrt)	Croom Helm	1983
I. Shaw & P. Nicholson	*B.M. Dictionary of Ancient Egypt*	B.M.P	1995

GREECE

Women of Ancient Greece

Jenifer Neils	*Women in the Ancient World*	B.M.P	2011
Dyfri Williams	*Women on Greek Vases* in *Images of Women in Antiquity* (EdA.Cameron & A. Kuhrt)	Croom Helm	1983

Women of Troy

Euripides	*Women of Troy*	Penguin Classics	1954

Medea

Euripides	*Medea*	Penguin Classics	1963

ROME

Women of Ancient Rome

Mary Beard	*SPQR*	Profile Books	2015
Jennifer Neils	*Women in the Ancient World*	BMP	2011

Cleopatra

Mary Beard	*Confronting the Classics*	Profile Books	2014
Plutarch	The lives of Julius Caesar & Mark Anthony in *Makers of Rome*	Penguin Classics	1965

Boudicca

Mary Beard	*Confronting the Classics*	Profile Books	2014
Tacitus	*Annals of Imperial Rome*	Penguin Classics	1956

Zenobia

N.G.L. Hammond & H.H. Scullard (Ed)	*Classical Dictionary*	O.U.P	1969
Pat Southern	*Empress Zenobia:*	Bloomsbury Academic	2009

THE 19TH AND 20TH CENTURIES

Amelia Edwards

Amelia B. Edwards	*A Thousand Miles Up the Nile*	Century Pub.	1982
T.G.H. James	*Excavating in Egypt*	B.M.P	1982

Gertrude Bell

Gertrude Bell	*The Desert and the Sown*	Cooper Square Pub.	1907
H.V.F. Winstone	*Gertrude Bell*	Hyperion Books	1984

WOMEN IN THE 21ST CENTURY

Hourig Sourouzian

Hourig Sourouzian

Egyptian Archaeology issues 39, 46, 50, 51 E.E.S

Penny Wilson

Penny Wilson   *Egyptian Archaeology* issues 12, 18   E.E.S

Amarna team

Anna Stevens et al *Horizon* Amarna Project & Amarna Trust Newsletter 2017

Map of the Ancient World

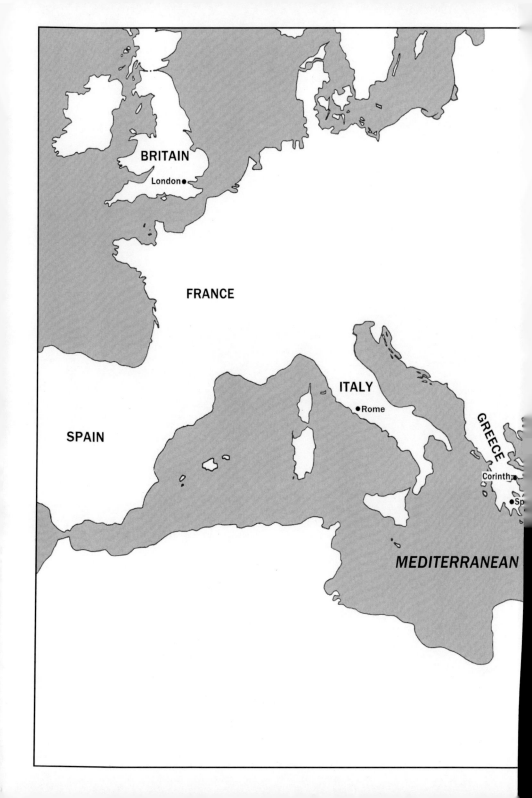